CONTENTS

PART ONE: INTRODUCING *NORTHANGER ABBEY*

PART TWO: STUDYING *NORTHANGER ABBEY*

PART THREE: CHARACTERS AND THEMES

PART FOUR: STRUCTURE, FORM AND LANGUAGE

PART FIVE: CONTEXTS AND CRITICAL DEBATES

PART SIX: GRADE BOOSTER

ESSENTIAL STUDY TOOLS

YORK NOTES

NORTHANGER ABBEY

JANE AUSTEN

Notes by Glennis Byron

Longman
is an imprint of

PEARSON

YORK
PRESS

YORK PRESS
322 Old Brompton Road, London SW5 9JH

PEARSON EDUCATION LIMITED
Edinburgh Gate, Harlow,
Essex CM20 2JE, United Kingdom

Associated companies, branches and representatives throughout the world

First published 2013

10 9 8 7 6 5 4 3 2 1

ISBN 978–1–4479–4885–8

Illustration on page 9 by Neil Gower
Phototypeset by Border Consultants
Printed in Italy

Photo credits:
© Classic Image/Alamy for page 6 / Bikeworldtravel/Shutterstock.com for page 7 / © Oxford Picture Library/Alamy for page 8 / ITV/Rex Features for page 10 / kuleczka/ Shutterstock.com for page 11 / ©iStockphoto.com/Pillon for page 12 / © Jeff Morgan 16/Alamy for page 14 / Natalia Semenchenko/Shutterstock.com for page 15 / JeremyRichards/Shutterstock.com for page 18 / © Cultura Creative/Alamy for page 19 / ©iStockphoto.com/PaulaConnelly for page 20 / © PhotoAlto sas/Alamy for page 21 / © Pictorial Press Ltd/Alamy for page 22 / © Maurice Savage/Alamy for page 23 / ©iStockphoto.com/MmeEmil for page 24 / Marcin-linfernum/Shutterstock.com for page 25 / Mariait/Shutterstock.com for page 26 /French School/Getty Images for page 27 / © V&A Images/Alamy for page 28 / © Steve Taylor ARPS/Alamy for page 31 / © The Art Archive/ Alamy for page 32 / James Osmond/Getty Images for page 33 / ©iStockphoto.com/belterz for page 34 / Melanie DeFazio/Shutterstock.com for page 35 / Calin Tatu/Shutterstock.com for page 36 / © Gianni Dagli Orti/Corbis for page 37 / © PhotoAlto sas/Alamy for page 38 / 1000 Words/Shutterstock.com for page 39 / © Kit Houghton/CORBIS for page 40 / Daphne Ma/Shutterstock.com for page 42 / ©iStockphoto.com/coloroftime for page 43 / ITV/Rex Features for page 44 / ©iStockphoto.com/genekrebs for page 46 / Thinkstock.com/ iStockphoto for page 47 / poo/Shutterstock.com for page 48 / Kenneth Dedeu/ Shutterstock.com for page 49 top / Kirk Mastin/Getty Images for page 49 bottom / Gavran333/Shutterstock.com for page 50 / Monbibi/Shutterstock.com for page 51/ ©iStockphoto.com/THEPALMER for page 52 / Chaloemphan/Shutterstock.com for page 53 / © Image Source/Alamy for page 54 / ©iStockphoto.com/Rihards for page 55 / ©iStockphoto.com/cotesebastien for page 57 / St. Nick/Shutterstock.com for page 58 / ©iStockphoto.com/TheDman for page 59 / Zbigniew Guzowski/Shutterstock.com for page 61 / © Robert Wilkinson/Alamy for page 63 / Kiselev Andrey Valerevich/Shutterstock.com for page 64 / ©Thinkstock.com/iStockphoto for page 65 / ©Thinkstock.com/Hemera for page 66 / DM7/Shutterstock.com for page 67 / ITV/Rex Features for page 68 top / ITV/Rex Features for page 68 bottom / ITV/Rex Features for page 70 / © PhotoAlto/Alamy for page 71 / ©Thinkstock.com/iStockphoto for page 72 / ©Thinkstock.com/Hemera for page 73 / ITV/Rex Features for page 74 / aGinger/Shutterstock.com for page 75 / ©iStockphoto.com/ graffoto8 for page 76 / ©iStockphoto.com/Akabei for page 77 / marekuliasz for page 78 / jannoon028/Shutterstock.com for page 79 top / Valeriy Lebedev/Shutterstock.com for page 79 middle / Discpicture/Shutterstock.com for page 80 bottom/ © Marc Sunderland/Alamy for page 82 / ©iStockphoto.com/PaulCalbar for page 83 / Matt Gibson/Shutterstock.com for page 84 / Voronin76/Shutterstock.com for page 85 / ©iStockphoto.com/Antagain for page 86 / © PhotoAlto/Alamy for page 88 / Suchan/Shutterstock.com for page 89 / © geogphotos/Alamy for page 90 / © EDIFICE/Alamy for page 91 / ©iStockphoto.com/ duncan1890 for page 92 / Neftali/Shutterstock.com for page 93 top / © North Wind Picture Archives/Alamy for page 93 bottom / Vitaly Korovin/Shutterstock.com for page 95 bottom

HOW TO STUDY *NORTHANGER ABBEY*

These Notes can be used in a range of ways to help you read, study and (where relevant) revise for your exam or assessment.

READING THE NOVEL

Read the novel once, fairly quickly, for pleasure. This will give you a good sense of the over-arching shape of the narrative, and a good feel for the highs and lows of the action, the pace and tone, and the sequence in which information is withheld or revealed. You could ask yourself:

- How do individual characters change or develop? How do my own responses to them change?
- From whose point of view is the novel told? Does this change or remain the same?
- Are the events presented chronologically, or is the time scheme altered in some way?
- What impression do the locations and settings, such as Bath and Northanger, make on my reading and response to the text?
- What sort of language, style and form am I aware of as the novel progresses? Does Austen structure the novel precisely, or is there a more relaxed approach – or both? Does she use **imagery**, or recurring **motifs** and **symbols**?

On your second reading, make detailed notes around the key areas highlighted above and in the Assessment Objectives, such as form, language, structure (AO2), links and connections to other texts (AO3) and the context/background for the novel (AO4). These may seem quite demanding, but these Notes will suggest particular elements to explore or jot down.

GRADE BOOSTER **A02**

Finding good quotations to support your interpretation of the characters will greatly enhance and strengthen your points.

INTERPRETING OR CRITIQUING THE NOVEL

Although it's not helpful to think in terms of the novel being 'good' or 'bad', you should consider the different ways the novel can be read. How have critics responded to it? Do their views match yours – or do you take a different viewpoint? Are there different ways you can interpret specific events, characters or settings? This is a key aspect in AO3, and it can be helpful to keep a log of your responses and the various perspectives which are expressed both by established critics, and also by classmates, your teacher or other readers.

CHECK THE BOOK **A01**

The 1992 York Handbook *Dictionary of Literary Terms*, by Martin Gray, provides explanations of the special vocabulary that will help you understand and write about novels like *Northanger Abbey*.

REFERENCES AND SOURCES

You will be expected to draw on critics' comments, or refer to source information from the period or the present. Make sure you make accurate, clear notes of writers or sources you have used, for example noting down titles of works, authors' names, website addresses, dates, etc. You may not have to reference all these things when you respond to a text, but knowing the source of your information will allow you to go back to it, if need be – and to check its accuracy and relevance.

REVISING FOR AND RESPONDING TO AN ASSESSED TASK OR EXAM QUESTION

The structure and the contents of these Notes are designed to give you the relevant information or ideas to answer tasks you have been set. First, work out the key words or ideas from the task (for example, 'form', 'language', 'Henry Tilney', etc.), then read the relevant parts of the Notes that relate to these terms, selecting what is useful for revision or written response. Then, turn to **Part Six: Grade Booster** for help in formulating your actual response.

NORTHANGER ABBEY IN CONTEXT

JANE AUSTEN: LIFE AND TIMES

1775 Jane Austen is born on 16 December, the second daughter and seventh child of the Reverend George Austen, rector of the village of Steventon in Hampshire, and Cassandra Leigh

1789 The storming of the Bastille and the start of the French Revolution

1787 Austen begins writing the short parodic pieces that compose her **juvenilia**

1793 Following the French Revolution Britain declares war on the new Republic

1799 Napoleon seizes control of the French government and the Napoleonic Wars begin – they continue until the battle of Waterloo in 1815

1801 George Austen retires and the family moves to Bath

1802 Austen receives a proposal of marriage from Harris Bigg-Wither, whom she had known since a child and who was heir to extensive estates. She accepts and then changes her mind the next day

1805 George Austen dies and Austen moves, with her mother and sister, first to Southampton and then, in 1809, to Chawton in Hampshire, where she remains for the rest of her life

1811 The illness of George III leads to the Prince of Wales being appointed Prince Regent and the period known as the 'Regency' begins

1817 After a year of bad health, Austen dies on 18 July in Winchester. Her brother Henry and sister Cassandra oversee the posthumous publication of *Northanger Abbey*

PUBLICATION HISTORY OF *NORTHANGER ABBEY*

Austen began writing what became *Northanger Abbey* in 1798 after a winter visit to Bath. 'Susan', as it was initially called, was sold to the London firm of Benjamin Crosby for £10 in 1803; it was advertised as being in press that year, but, for reasons unknown, not published. In 1809, an anonymous novel called *Susan* appeared, and Austen was prompted to write to Crosby asking about her novel; he offered to return the manuscript for the £10 he paid, and threatened legal action if it were published elsewhere. Austen presumably could not afford the £10 and did not buy back the manuscript at the time. After publishing *Sense and Sensibility* (1811), *Pride and Prejudice* (1813), *Mansfield Park* (1814) and *Emma* (1816), Austen had her brother Henry negotiate once more with the publisher, and recovered the manuscript. In light of the publication of the other *Susan*, Austen changed her heroine's name to Catherine and wrote a preface (the 'Advertisement') explaining the history of its publication; however, she made no attempt to publish it elsewhere before she died in 1817. Following her death, Henry and her sister Cassandra arranged for the publication of the novel, which they called *Northanger Abbey*. Henry wrote a 'Biographical Notice of the Author', in which Jane Austen was publicly named for the first time as the author of her novels. Along with *Persuasion*, also unpublished at the time of Austen's death, *Northanger Abbey* appeared in December 1817, with an official publication date of 1818.

THE WORLD OF AUSTEN'S NOVELS

Until the 1970s, Austen was seen as a genteel spinster and as a highly conservative and quintessentially English writer, part of a 'chocolate-box' England of rose-covered cottages. She was considered to have little interest in the politics of her age, and to focus on a very limited world. Her own description of her work in a letter to her nephew James Austen, dated as 16 December 1816, as a 'little bit (two Inches wide) of Ivory on which I work with so fine a Brush', in was often cited in support of such a position. While this is still the impression often given by the heritage film industry in adapting Austen's works, it is no longer the dominant critical perspective. Marilyn Butler in *Jane Austen and the War of Ideas* (1975) was the first to contest this view, arguing that even if she did not appear to address directly such topics as the Napoleonic Wars and the Industrial Revolution, Austen was nevertheless subtly engaged with the controversies of her class and her generation. *Northanger Abbey* is certainly neither apolitical nor ahistorical, as will be suggested throughout these Notes (see also **Part Five: Historical Background**).

RANK

Social position or 'rank' – a word differing from our modern idea of class in being more defined by birthright than by productivity and income – is of central importance to Austen's novels. She has little concern with either the aristocracy or the labouring classes, and is concerned mainly with the rural gentry, that is, those of the rank of 'gentleman' who were independent landowners. Many of these landowners had become even wealthier through the enclosure system, which gave them restricted rights over what was previously common land. The society Austen depicts ranges mainly from these major landowners (like General Tilney, who has benefited from enclosure, or Mr Darcy in *Pride and Prejudice*) down to the upper professional classes closely linked to the gentry (sometimes called the 'pseudo' gentry) including clergymen, barristers and officers in the army and navy, those who were still considered 'gentlemen' and yet did not derive their income from land.

WEALTH

Wealth is also central in Austen's world. Money is needed to acquire all the material goods that signal one's claim to a particular station in life. Austen is often quite specific about how much a character has inherited, or how much that character's annual income might be from investments. But if the detail is missing, the markers of the income are clear. The house, the furnishings, the number of servants and the type (if any) of carriage, all these would have been signals to Austen's contemporaries about the status of the owner. Women, of course, were prevented by law from having any real control over money, and they could not inherit land. In a society where she cannot work – at least not if she wants to retain her status – where there are no benefits and no governmental pensions, a woman needs to be able to access money through marriage if she is not, like Austen herself, to remain dependent on her own family throughout her life.

MORALS AND MANNERS

For Austen, morality is intricately tied up with action, that is, one is judged by what one does and not what one feels. Morally upright behaviour is consequently allied with what in Austen's world could be called 'manners' or 'propriety'. It means being sensitive to the needs of others rather than simply pursuing one's own interests. Seen in this light, social forms and conventions are not restrictions on personal freedom, but a way of ensuring proper conduct and respect for others. This is best encapsulated in *Northanger Abbey* by the character of Eleanor, whose good breeding is set in direct opposition to the self-serving Isabella.

CONSUMER CULTURE

Rapid industrialisation had produced a huge increase in urban populations, and increasing affluence among the growing middle classes meant an increased demand for luxury goods. Commodities were imported from all over the world, and improved transport systems meant they were available throughout the country. There was a resulting expansion in the number of shops. While traditionally goods had been purchased in fairs and markets, England was well on its way to becoming, in the phrase first used by Adam Smith in *The Wealth of Nations* (1776) but made famous by Napoleon I, a 'nation of shopkeepers'.

CHECK THE FILM A03

There have been only two film adaptations of *Northanger Abbey*: the 2007 Granada version directed by Jon Jones and written by Andrew Davies, and the 1987 BBC version directed by Giles Foster and written by Maggie Wadey. Victor Nunez's *Ruby in Paradise* (1993) is a very loose updated adaptation.

CONTEXT A04

The precarious financial position of women explains why the courtship and marriage plot is so central to Austen's works, and why the lives of many mothers, like Mrs Thorpe in *Northanger Abbey* and Mrs Bennet in *Pride and Prejudice*, revolve around getting daughters married.

BATH

The greater part of the novel is set in Bath, the most important and most elegant of the spa towns, and a clear example of the rise of a consumer culture. By the end of the eighteenth century, apart from the 30,000 full-time residents, there were around 40,000 visitors each season. In addition to being a health spa with health-giving waters, Bath offered a range of public entertainments, including concerts, theatre, balls, dinners, pleasure gardens and gala nights with spectacular fireworks. The streets were full of sumptuous shops, with large windows displaying tempting goods. Milsom Street in particular was already famed as a shopping centre. The public assemblies, either those in the Lower Rooms in the older part of town, or the Upper Rooms in the newer, offered dancing, card games and tea, and were presided over by a master of ceremonies who ensured certain regulations were followed and made introductions. Bath was, above all, very much a marriage market, where eligible young men and women went to see and be seen.

SENTIMENTAL AND GOTHIC ROMANCES

Northanger Abbey **parodies** both the sentimental **romance** (in Volume One) and the **Gothic** romance (in Volume Two). The typical plot structures of the two **genres** are similar, dealing primarily with the heroine's entry into the wider world and her attempt to achieve a happy marriage. Sentimental romance, exemplified by such works as Samuel Richardson's tragic *Clarissa, or the History of a Young Lady* (1748) and the **satiric** social comedy of Frances Burney's *Evelina; or the History of a Young Lady's Entrance into the World* (1778), features young women whose excessive feelings are aligned with virtue and who are subjected to persecution at the hands of domineering men. They are frequently written in the form of letters or journals, allowing for an emphasis on the emotions of the heroine, and end in either a happy and advantageous marriage, as in the case of *Evelina*, or in death, as in the case of *Clarissa*. (See also **Part Five: Literary Background**.)

In the late eighteenth century, the Gothic novelist Ann Radcliffe and her followers restaged the sentimental heroine, taking her out of the contemporary world, and placing her within past times. In Radcliffean romance, the heroine is removed from the safety of her home, often by the death of parents, and propelled into the wider world. The country or town house of sentimental romance gives way to ruined castles or abbeys in the Alps or Pyrenees. Instead of being persecuted by the cruel father and the libertine, the Gothic heroine is usually threatened by aristocratic tyrants or banditti. The threat is variously to their honour and to their inheritances. Finally, the heroine's fears are often intensified by the apparent presence of the supernatural, something that Radcliffe and her followers usually explain away. (See also **Part Four: Form**, on **Gothic**).

CHARACTERS IN *NORTHANGER ABBEY*

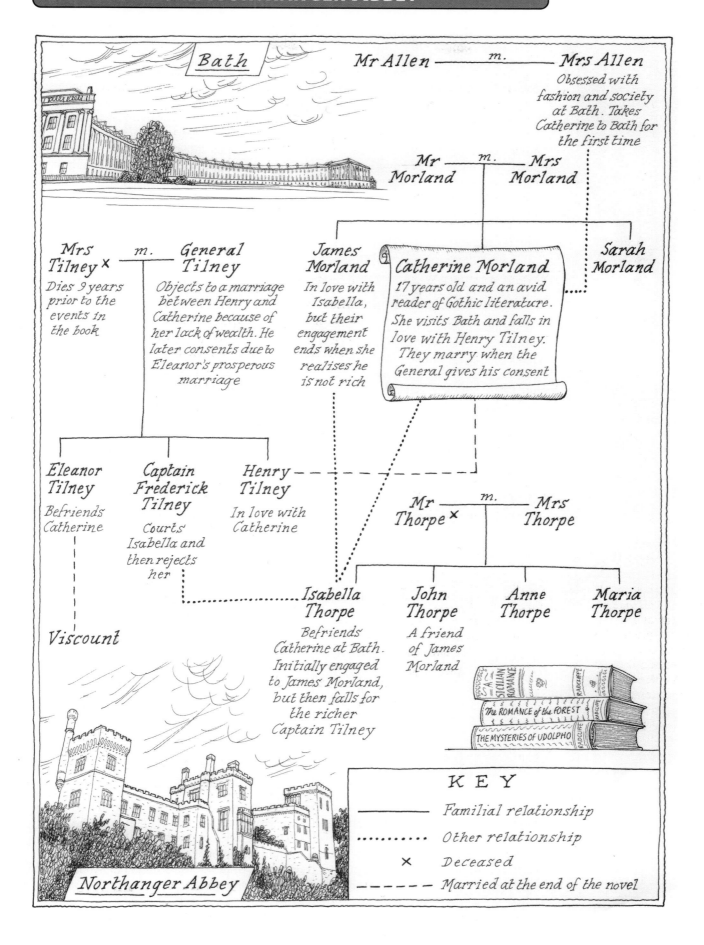

Bath

Mr Allen — m. — Mrs Allen
Obsessed with fashion and society at Bath. Takes Catherine to Bath for the first time

Mr Morland — m. — Mrs Morland

Mrs Tilney ✕ — m. — General Tilney
Dies 9 years prior to the events in the book

Objects to a marriage between Henry and Catherine because of her lack of wealth. He later consents due to Eleanor's prosperous marriage

James Morland
In love with Isabella, but their engagement ends when she realises he is not rich

Catherine Morland
17 years old and an avid reader of Gothic literature. She visits Bath and falls in love with Henry Tilney. They marry when the General gives his consent

Sarah Morland

Eleanor Tilney
Befriends Catherine

Captain Frederick Tilney
Courts Isabella and then rejects her

Henry Tilney
In love with Catherine

Mr Thorpe ✕ — m. — Mrs Thorpe

Viscount

Isabella Thorpe
Befriends Catherine at Bath. Initially engaged to James Morland, but then falls for the richer Captain Tilney

John Thorpe
A friend of James Morland

Anne Thorpe

Maria Thorpe

A SICILIAN ROMANCE — RADCLIFFE
The ROMANCE of the FOREST — RADCLIFFE
THE MYSTERIES OF UDOLPHO — RADCLIFFE

KEY
——— Familial relationship
·········· Other relationship
✕ Deceased
- - - - - Married at the end of the novel

Northanger Abbey

SYNOPSIS

THE HEROINE'S ADVENTURES BEGIN

The **narrator** introduces her unlikely heroine, Catherine Morland, with an account of Catherine's very ordinary childhood and exceedingly normal family. At seventeen, Catherine is invited by her wealthy neighbours, Mr and Mrs Allen, to accompany them to Bath. Catherine is excited by the idea but, on arriving there, she is initially disappointed because the Allens have no acquaintance in Bath. One evening, she is formally introduced to the witty Henry Tilney, a respectable clergyman from a good family in Gloucestershire. Mrs Allen also meets an old school friend, Mrs Thorpe, a widow with financial problems. Over the next few days, Catherine becomes friends with Mrs Thorpe's beautiful eldest daughter, Isabella. Henry, meanwhile, is nowhere to be seen.

EDUCATING CATHERINE

Isabella introduces Catherine to the delights of Ann Radcliffe's *The Mysteries of Udolpho*, and promises they will read many more **Gothic** novels together. The two girls encounter Isabella's brother John and Catherine's brother James in the streets of Bath. It emerges that, as John's friend, James has visited the Thorpe family during the holidays and is already quite infatuated with Isabella. She in turn clearly has designs on him, while the boastful John begins to pursue Catherine. Catherine is persuaded to go for a drive in John's gig and Mrs Allen demonstrates her inadequacies as a guardian by failing to point out the impropriety of such an excursion. Catherine increasingly dislikes John, whose speech is peppered with profanities and who talks constantly of horses and carriages and drink. At the same time she increasingly likes the witty Henry, who has returned to Bath, and whose elegance and **ironic** style she finds fascinating if strange. She meets Henry's sister Eleanor.

CATHERINE'S EDUCATION CONTINUES

Henry again asks Catherine to dance, and he is annoyed by John Thorpe's attempt to interfere. Catherine, Henry and Eleanor make plans to go for a walk the next day. Catherine is deceived by John Thorpe into thinking the Tilneys are not coming and, tempted by the idea of visiting Blaise Castle, persuaded into another excursion. Catherine sees the Tilneys walking towards her from the carriage, but John refuses to stop. The walk with the Tilneys eventually takes place after Catherine firmly refuses to go with James and the Thorpes on yet one more trip. The Tilneys and Catherine go to Beechen Cliff and they talk of such matters as language, novels, history and the **picturesque**. Catherine is delighted to be asked to dine with the Tilneys. The next day, Isabella tells her that she is engaged to James. Mr Morland's consent is given. John Thorpe attempts to court Catherine with little success.

ENTER TWO VILLAINS

The dinner with the Tilneys is not a success. Eleanor and Henry seem restrained in the company of their father General Tilney, and Catherine, despite the General's polite attentions, is ill at ease. Henry's elder brother Captain Tilney comes to the ball the next evening, and Catherine is horrified when Isabella agrees to dance with him. James, meanwhile, has been to see his father, and returns with news concerning the income he may expect on his marriage. Isabella is visibly disappointed in the amount. Catherine is invited to visit the Tilneys' home, Northanger Abbey, and her mind is immediately filled with Gothic visions. At the same time, however, she is increasingly disturbed by the developing flirtation between Isabella and Captain Tilney.

GRADE BOOSTER A02

While plot summary is the point of a synopsis, it should not be part of your essay. Always assume your reader knows the story and focus instead on your analysis of that story.

CHECK THE BOOK A04

Juliet McMaster's *Jane Austen and Love* (1978) offers an analysis of the relationship between the heroes as mentor-lovers and the heroines they educate.

GOTHIC IMAGININGS

Catherine journeys to Northanger with the Tilneys, first in the General's ostentatious coach and four with Eleanor and then, for the second part of the journey, in Henry's smaller carriage, a curricle. Henry teases her with a **parody** of a Gothic tale: he makes Catherine the heroine of the story and elaborates what she might find at Northanger. Catherine is immediately disappointed by the modern appearance of the abbey. Left in her room to dress, she spots an immense heavy chest, which starts her fantasising about its possibly dreadful contents. When she finally opens the chest, it contains nothing but a white bedspread, and she is ashamed of her absurd expectations. Later that night, she sees a black cabinet resembling the one in Henry's story. She finds in a secret place what she assumes is a manuscript but must wait for daylight to read it. It turns out to be a series of washing bills. Catherine next begins to be suspicious of the General and the fate of the supposedly late Mrs Tilney. She eventually goes exploring and finds Mrs Tilney's room but there is no evidence of foul play. She is caught by Henry, who laughs at her for what he considers her absurd fancies and encourages her to consider the nature of the country – England – in which she lives: a world of laws and light, of reason and security.

HORRORS IN THE MIDLAND COUNTIES OF ENGLAND

Catherine determines to be more sensible. She starts to wonder why she has not heard from Isabella. A letter arrives from James telling her that the engagement is over and the reason lies with Captain Tilney. Catherine assumes Captain Tilney and Isabella are to be married, but Henry and Eleanor think this unlikely. Catherine, Eleanor and the General go to Woodston to dine with Henry at his parsonage. Catherine finds this a pastoral paradise and much preferable to the grandeur of the abbey. She then receives a letter from Isabella, who has clearly been let down by Captain Tilney and is looking to find a way to get James back. Catherine finally sees through her and does not respond. The General goes to London and Henry to Woodston, but one night the General returns in a fury and orders Catherine to be ejected from the house the next morning. Eleanor does not understand why and explains she cannot prevent it. Catherine returns home, humiliated and despondent.

HAPPILY EVER AFTER

A few days later Henry arrives. He asks her to marry him and she accepts. Henry explains that John Thorpe had persuaded the General that Catherine was to be the heir of the wealthy Allens, and when the General found out the truth, he had her thrown out. The Morlands give their consent to the marriage of Henry and Catherine but insist that they get the consent of the General. While this seems unlikely, Eleanor makes an advantageous match with the young man she loves who has conveniently inherited the wealth and title that allow him to marry her. The General is delighted enough to grudgingly give his consent to the marriage of Henry and Catherine.

CONTEXT **A04**

'Take – An old castle, half of it ruinous.
A long gallery, with a great many doors, some secret ones.
Three murdered bodies, quite fresh.
As many skeletons, in chests and presses.
An old woman hanging by the neck; with her throat cut.
Assassins and desperados …
Noise, whispers and groans, threescore at least.
Mix them together, in the form of three volumes, to be taken at any of the watering places before going to bed.'

(Recipe for Gothic novel, *Walkers Hibernian Magazine*, January 1778)

VOLUME ONE, CHAPTER 1

SUMMARY

- The **narrator** introduces Catherine Morland with a description of her as a plain and unexceptional child and suggests her unsuitability for the role of heroine.
- At fifteen, Catherine's appearance improves and she begins to educate herself for the role of heroine.
- The Morlands' childless and wealthy neighbours, Mr and Mrs Allen, invite Catherine to accompany them to Bath.

ANALYSIS

READERS AND READING

Northanger Abbey, as we'll see throughout these Notes, is very much a novel about reading: the way in which one reads and the effects of one's reading. In the beginning, Catherine is an unsophisticated reader. She has nothing against books, the narrator **ironically** observes, as long as they serve no useful function and remain 'all story and no reflection' (p. 17). In addition, when 'in training for a heroine' (p. 17), she chooses books of extracts that allow for the fast and superficial acquisition of literary knowledge. An example of such books would be Vicesimus Knox's *Elegant Extracts: Useful and Entertaining Passages in Prose* (1797). Catherine has to learn to be a discerning reader, both of books and of people. However, it is not just Catherine but also the more general use of literature for profit and self-display that is the target of Austen's **satire** here.

PARODYING THE HEROINE

Northanger Abbey is often described as a **parody** (a satiric imitation) of the **romance**, particularly the **Gothic** romance, and the heroines of such novels. Catherine, it is worth noting, is the only one of Austen's female **protagonists** that she describes with the term 'heroine'. Indeed, Austen uses the word 'heroine' only twenty-six times in total in her novels, and twenty-four of these occurrences are in *Northanger Abbey*. The idea of the heroine, therefore, is clearly of some importance here.

In describing all the things that Catherine is not, Austen draws on – and expects her readers to recognise – many **tropes** common to the heroine of Gothic romance. Such a heroine will often have a dead or absent mother, a dead, absent, or alternatively inattentive, even cruel father. She is beautiful and accomplished, with a well-developed appreciation of nature. She will be forced into a series of adventures, separated from her lover, betrayed by her guardian and persecuted by some brooding aristocratic villain.

Consider how Catherine repeatedly fails to meet the supposed 'standards' of such heroines. In terms of accomplishments, for example, Catherine may draw, but she draws only 'houses and trees, hens and chickens, all very much like one another' (p. 16). Nevertheless, it is not Catherine that is being attacked here. Though naive and unsophisticated, Catherine seems to have a relatively healthy and normal childhood. Rather, Austen parodies and attacks the over-exaggerated virtues and adventures of the traditional sentimental heroine of romance.

STUDY FOCUS: AUSTEN'S NARRATOR A02

No other Austen narrator imposes herself on the reader quite so much as the narrator of *Northanger Abbey*. The **intrusive narrative** 'I' appears very rarely in *Pride and Prejudice* (1813), *Sense and Sensibility* (1811) and *Persuasion* (1818) and never in *Emma* (1815). In this opening chapter, the narrator cultivates a relationship with the reader, assuming we have similar tastes and intelligence, and to some extent distancing us from her heroine and inviting us to smile at Catherine. Note how this is quite different from making Catherine the target of the satiric attack.

The narrative voice is witty, opinionated, intrusive and self-conscious: that is, the narrator is clear and open from the start that this is a novel, and that she is the 'contriver', as she later describes herself (p. 217), of the fiction we read. Such a narrator is sometimes described as an **authorial narrator**. This does not mean that we should assume that the author, Jane Austen, and the narrator are one and the same – always avoid calling the narrator 'Austen'. Rather, it is a reference to the narrator's assumption of a position of privilege, a sense of the narrator's control or ownership of the world described, made clear by extensive commentaries upon characters or issues.

CHECK THE BOOK A03

You will find some modern and updated versions of the authorial narrator in such short stories by Angela Carter as 'The Company of Wolves'.

GLOSSARY

16   **'Beggar's Petition'** a highly sentimental and pathetic poem by the Reverend Thomas Moss, often given to children to learn and recite

16   **'The Hare and many Friends'** originally one of Aesop's Fables and rewritten in the form of a poem by John Gay (1727). The theme of false friends **foreshadows** Catherine's relationship with Isabella

KEY QUOTATIONS: VOLUME ONE, CHAPTER 1 A01

Key quotation 1: 'No one who had ever seen Catherine Morland in her infancy, would have supposed her born to be an heroine' (p. 15).

Possible interpretations:

- Implies that despite her unsuitability, Catherine will become a heroine.
- The use of 'seen', instead of, for example, 'known', introduces the importance of the visual in the novel and the possible deceptiveness of appearances.
- 'Heroine' refers not to qualities of courage or daring, but to the principal female character in a work of fiction, and more specifically the romance, therefore suggesting the importance of books and reading.

Key quotation 2: 'Something must and will happen to throw a hero in her way' (p. 18).

Possible interpretations:

- Foreshadows the meeting with Henry Tilney in Bath.
- Draws attention to the **self-conscious narrator** who will be the one to provide the hero.
- Exemplifies the narrator's parodic tone when speaking of heroes and heroines.

CHECK THE FILM A03

Northanger Abbey has never had the Hollywood treatment. Journalist Maureen Dowd, reflecting on the popularity of Jane Austen films in 1995, suggested that Hollywood *could* film *Northanger Abbey*, but the movie would have 'Sandra Bullock as *Abbey Northanger*, a governess who falls for a ghost' (*New York Times*, 24 August 1995: A23). Why do you think this is?

VOLUME ONE, CHAPTER 2

SUMMARY

- Catherine accompanies Mr and Mrs Allen to Bath.
- They attend a ball in the Upper Rooms but the evening is not a success.
- They have no acquaintances amongst the huge crowds and Catherine consequently has no dance partner.

ANALYSIS

THE HEROINE'S GUARDIAN

CHECK THE BOOK A03

In Ann Radcliffe's *Mysteries of Udolpho*, a novel soon to become Catherine's favourite, the orphaned heroine Emily is the ward of her aunt, Madame Cheron, who mistreats her and confiscates her property, leading her to become the prisoner of the villain Montoni.

Heroines of romances, particularly **Gothic** romances, are frequently orphans and placed in the hands of ineffectual or even actively malicious guardians. Austen **parodies** this convention with Mrs Allen, a woman with 'a great deal of quiet, inactive good temper, and a trifling turn of mind' (p. 21). Concerned primarily with shopping and with fine clothes, Mrs Allen seems very unlikely to 'promote the general distress of the work' (p. 20) since she will probably not cause the problems we expect the Gothic heroine to experience.

And yet, despite the narrator's apparent **irony** here, Mrs Allen will actually be at least partly responsible for a number of Catherine's problems, and in some ways anticipates another somewhat difficult character: Mrs Bennet in the later *Pride and Prejudice*. Inept as a chaperone, the empty-headed Mrs Allen may teach Catherine all about the latest fashions (three or four days are spent on this), but she fails to guide Catherine in matters of propriety, of what is and is not appropriate behaviour for a young girl. Mr Allen too, although more sensible than his wife and more aware of his responsibilities, is sometimes, perhaps understandably, too eager to avoid Mrs Allen's company. In this chapter he escapes to the card room, leaving the two women to fend for themselves in the crowded ballroom.

CHECK THE BOOK A04

There are many useful sources of information on clothes and fashion in Jane Austen's time. See for example Antje Blank's essay on 'Dress' in Janet Todd's *Jane Austen in Context* (2005). For a wealth of illustrations, see Sarah Jane Downing's *Fashion in the Time of Jane Austen* (2011).

STUDY FOCUS: A PASSION FOR DRESS A02

As Jane Austen's letters to her sister Cassandra reveal, she was a keen follower of fashion, and this interest is particularly evident here. None of Austen's other novels devotes quite as much attention to dress as *Northanger Abbey*. Clothes, and attitudes towards clothes, play a significant role in characterisation, a theme introduced here through Mrs Allen: 'Dress was her passion', the **narrator** observes, 'She had a most harmless delight in being fine' (p. 21). Is it, however, completely harmless? As you read the novel, notice how frequently Mrs Allen refers to problems of dress when there are far more important matters at stake (see for example pp. 99 and 222) and how her judgements of people are frequently and shallowly based on the evidence dress provides of wealth or class (see for example p. 31).

CONSUMER CULTURE

One of the key moments in the development of our modern consumer culture was the expansion of the marketplace, the explosion of consumer choices produced by the Industrial Revolution and the wider penetration of consumer goods into the lives of people of very different social classes. The gentry, middle and working classes all adopted the values of a consumer culture: goods acquired social significance. Consumption, according to many critics, was also prompted by a new sense of fashion and taste and by the development of shopping, advertising and marketing.

One of Austen's main concerns in *Northanger Abbey* is the growth of this consumer culture, and Bath is the ideal setting for the exploration of this theme. Bath was the most fashionable city of the late eighteenth century. It was not just a spa town where people flocked to drink the supposedly health-giving waters, it was also a place for leisure activities, dancing, gambling, concerts and theatre, and for shopping. The city had recently undergone a thorough renovation programme and rows of shops set out tempting merchandise. Bath's association with commodities, however, extends well beyond this. It was a place to see and be seen and, as Isabella will make clear in the next chapters, it was an unofficial marriage market, with the assemblies offering the opportunity for meeting potential partners, and most convenient for those with an eye on a title or a fortune.

STUDY FOCUS: THE TRAVELLING HEROINE [A02]

Once again, Austen parodies the conventions of the Gothic **romance** with her description of the highly uneventful journey to Bath. There are no storms, no robbers and no accidents with the carriage. The most alarming event is the possible loss of a pair of clogs. Compare this with the 'journey' Mrs Allen and Catherine make through the 'struggling assembly' that evening in the Upper Rooms (p. 21). Language here suggests almost insuperable difficulties. It is a journey requiring 'unwearied diligence' (p. 22) to reach the top of the room; here is only disappointment as they still can see nothing but some of the high feathers of the ladies dancing. Only by a 'continued exertion of strength and ingenuity' do they reach a prospect where they gain a 'comprehensive view' of the assembly below (p. 22). The language ironically links the movement through the room to the ascent of a mountain, but the prospect they gain is a 'splendid sight' not of landscape, but of dancers. What other language can you find that makes the connection between ascending a room and a mountain in this passage?

GLOSSARY

20	**Pulteney-street**	the widest, grandest and most elegant street in Bath
21	**Upper Rooms**	the newest and largest assembly rooms, built to cater to those in the newer and higher part of town; balls were held twice a week and would attract anywhere from 800 to 1,200 guests at the height of the season

CONTEXT [A04]

Both *Northanger Abbey* and *Persuasion* are set primarily in Bath. Highlighting some of the landmarks mentioned in these novels, Bath Tourism offers a free online MP3 Audio Walking Tour of Bath that includes extracts from Austen's letters and the novels.

CHECK THE BOOK [A03]

Don Slater's *Consumer Culture and Modernity* (1997) offers an accessible discussion of the growth of consumer culture.

VOLUME ONE, CHAPTER 3

SUMMARY

- Catherine and the Allens attend a ball in the Lower Rooms.
- Catherine is introduced to Henry Tilney by the master of ceremonies.
- Tilney is a clergyman from a respectable and wealthy family in Gloucestershire.
- Catherine is very attracted to Tilney, and he endears himself to Mrs Allen with his detailed knowledge of muslins.

ANALYSIS

CRITICAL VIEWPOINT A03

Some critics suggest that the discussion about muslins is an example of the way Henry is somewhat feminised, while others argue his ability to indulge in such 'girl talk' signals that he will make a good companionable husband.

A MATTER OF MUSLIN

Until the end of the eighteenth century, formal clothing for fashionable men and women was made of silk, satin or velvet. The common use of lace around the neck or sleeves was partly because lace was washable, while the other materials were not. From 1721 to 1774 cotton textiles had been banned in order to protect the silk industry, and while cotton was imported and manufactured in England after this, real Indian muslin was always considered the most elegant and desirable. Mrs Allen, it should be noted, has actually been vastly overcharged for her muslin, as Austen's contemporaries would have known. And Henry Tilney is quite an unusual hero for an Austen novel in his ability to discuss the price and quality of muslins, another example of Austen's rewriting of clichés and stereotypes.

STUDY FOCUS: THE RULES OF THE GAME — A04

CONTEXT A04

'In the morning the rendezvous is at the Pump-Room; from that time 'till noon in walking on the Parades or … visiting the shops; thence to the Pump-Room again, and after a fresh strole, to dinner; and from dinner to the Theatre … or the Rooms, where dancing, or the card-table, concludes the evening' (Christopher Anstey, *The New Bath Guide, or, Useful Pocket Companion,* 1799).

Bath was known for certain freedoms, including a relaxed attitude towards rank. Nevertheless, a set of rules did regulate behaviour, some of which would be posted by the master of ceremonies on the assembly room walls. The assemblies combined dancing with cards, tea and conversation, and, for the young, offered an education in social intercourse. Earlier in the century, the famous master of ceremonies Beau Nash had initiated these rules in his attempt to refine and civilise the rural gentry. Swords had to be left at the door, for example, and no boots or leather breeches were permitted. There were also strict rules about dancing and etiquette. Catherine is unable to dance the first evening because one had to be properly introduced to one's partner. Activities were also strictly regulated. The balls began at six o'clock. At nine o'clock, the gentlemen would treat their partners to tea: no partner usually meant no tea. At eleven o'clock on the dot the master of ceremonies would order the music to cease.

There were also conventions determining polite social interaction, and Henry Tilney pokes fun at these as he tests Catherine's knowledge of the schedule of activities to be followed. Henry, like Austen herself, is indulging in **parody**: as Austen parodies the rules of a **genre**, so he parodies the rules of a society. In the Introduction to the Penguin Classics edition, Marilyn Butler calls Henry the 'Master of Games' (p. xli), and suggests that Catherine quickly understands how to play the game while Mrs Allen does not. What evidence from this chapter could you offer to support this argument?

GLOSSARY

25	**Pump-room**	where all went to see and be seen, and to drink the spa water
25	**Lower Rooms**	smaller assembly rooms near the Avon river, used during the day for promenading and for evening balls twice a week

VOLUME ONE, CHAPTER 4

SUMMARY

- The next day, Catherine eagerly looks forward to seeing Henry Tilney, but he is nowhere to be found.
- Mrs Allen meets an old school friend, the widow Mrs Thorpe, who is in Bath with her three daughters.
- Catherine remembers that her brother James is a friend of Mrs Thorpe's son, John, and had spent a week with the Thorpe family in the Christmas holidays.
- Catherine is delighted to gain a new friend in the eldest daughter, Isabella.

ANALYSIS

FRIENDSHIP

Austen shows the beginnings of two friendships in this chapter. The first, between Mrs Allen and Mrs Thorpe, is viewed **satirically**, with underlying motivations made quite clear. Mrs Thorpe needs an audience for her endless commentary on her children while Mrs Allen needs an acquaintance, particularly one to whom she can feel superior in terms of dress. The second friendship, between Catherine and Isabella, initially appears to be a more genuine and promising friendship, based on affection rather than self-interest. Nevertheless, the **narrator**'s satiric remarks on the swiftness with which affection grows and the pointed reference to Mrs Thorpe's lack of money should make the reader wary. As we'll soon realise, Isabella has probably planned this trip to Bath specifically to meet and befriend Catherine, whose brother James she believes to be a good catch.

STUDY FOCUS: EDUCATING CATHERINE — A02

Austen spends the first few chapters emphasising her heroine's simplicity and naivety, but by the end of the novel Catherine will have grown and developed as a result of her experiences. Catherine has now made the acquaintance of two very different families, the Thorpes and the Tilneys, and she will learn through her interactions with them, both in Bath and at Northanger Abbey. Part of her education is to discern and assess the differences in the characters, ambitions and values of these two families. This emphasis on a movement from naivety to knowledge identifies the novel as a form of **Bildungsroman**, or coming-of-age narrative. As you read through the novel, identify more specifically the kinds of lessons that Catherine learns.

It could be argued that the novel is actually more about education than **romance**. *Northanger Abbey* focuses less on the obstacles between lovers central to the progress of traditional romance narratives, and more on Catherine's growing social and moral awareness. What specific evidence might support or conflict with such a reading?

GLOSSARY

30	**despair of nothing we would attain**	lines from Thomas Dyche, *A Guide to the English Tongue* (1707)
31	**pelisse**	a long coat with or without sleeves, and often trimmed or lined with fur
32	**quizzes**	the word 'quiz', first recorded in 1782, was originally used as a noun and meant an odd or eccentric person

CHECK THE BOOK — A03

The character of Isabella Thorpe precedes the equally manipulative husband-hunter Lucy Steele in Austen's *Sense and Sensibility*, who professes instant affection for Elinor. Such obviously false friendships indicate unreliable and dishonest characters in Austen. One might think too of Caroline Bingley in *Pride and Prejudice* and her clearly false affection for Jane Bennet.

CHECK THE BOOK — A03

Other notable examples of Bildungsroman include Charlotte Brontë's *Jane Eyre* (1847) and Charles Dickens's *Great Expectations* (1861). Many of the stories in Angela Carter's *The Bloody Chamber* (1979), including the title story, are forms of Bildungsroman.

VOLUME ONE, CHAPTER 5

SUMMARY

- Catherine continues to look in vain for Mr Tilney.
- The friendship between Catherine and Isabella grows more intimate. They are constantly in each other's company and on rainy days read novels together.
- The chapter concludes with a defence of the novel.

ANALYSIS

DEFENCE OF THE NOVEL

The defence of the novel and of women novelists in particular is the longest narrative digression in any of Austen's works, and to understand this need to recognise the changes in the literary world at the time. Publishing boomed in the eighteenth century and there was an accompanying rise in literacy, leading to the emergence of professional authors who wrote for the market. Literature became a business and novels were central to this. Notice how often the language in this section reflects Austen's recognition that books are commodities. Partly because they were market-centred, novels, though providing 'more extensive and unaffected pleasure than those of any other literary corporation in the world' (p. 36), were still often disparaged as trash, and the 'labour' of novelists undervalued (p. 36). For a more detailed discussion, see **Part Five: Historical Background**.

Even the novelists themselves frequently apologised for their choice of **genre**, a gesture Austen calls an 'ungenerous and impolitic custom' (p. 36). She argues that contemporary novels, full of wit and humour and revealing a deep knowledge of human nature, are far superior to the out-dated ideas and unnatural characters found in collections of such older works as the *Spectator* magazine. In light of Austen's defence of the novel, be alert throughout to the ways in which characters reveal themselves by their attitudes towards reading: you might compare, for example, John Thorpe's rejection of novels (p. 47) and Henry Tilney's appreciation of them (pp. 102–3) in the context of the **narrator**'s argument here.

STUDY FOCUS: FREE INDIRECT STYLE A01

After church on Sunday morning, we learn, the Thorpes and Allens 'stayed long enough in the Pump-room to discover that the crowd was insupportable, and that there was not a genteel face to be seen' and so they 'hastened away to the Crescent, to breathe the fresh air of better company' (p. 34). Whose perspective are we being offered in these lines, that of the narrator or that of the characters?

This is an example of a narrative technique for which Austen is much celebrated: **free indirect style**. The vocabulary used in the example here – 'the crowd was insupportable', 'not a genteel face to be seen' – suggests the kind of overstatement we associate with Isabella. However, when we know that the Crescent is the particular haunt of the rich and fashionable, then the fact that the characters hasten 'to breathe the fresh air of better company' introduces the **satiric** perspective of the narrator at the same time, in showing Isabella's real motivation.

Free indirect style is not used in *Northanger Abbey* to the same extent as in the later novels, as here Austen generally uses an **intrusive narrator** who participates much more directly. Nevertheless, it is important to keep your eye open for other early examples of free indirect discourse (see also **Part Four: Language**, on **Free indirect discourse**).

VOLUME ONE, CHAPTER 6

SUMMARY

- Catherine and Isabella have a conversation about books and about men.
- Isabella hints to the oblivious Catherine that she is attracted to Catherine's brother James.
- The two set off in pursuit of two young men Isabella supposedly wants to avoid.

ANALYSIS

MISTRESS OF CEREMONIES

In her introduction to the Penguin Classics edition of *Northanger Abbey* (1995), Marilyn Butler describes Isabella as 'temporarily Mistress of Ceremonies' (p. xli), and 'the conspirator who at Bath controls the threads of the plot' (p. xl). There are, however, some limits to the degree to which she can manipulate Catherine in this chapter, simply because Catherine is too naive to recognise the games that Isabella is trying to play. Here, while Catherine tries to talk about books, Isabella unsuccessfully attempts to reveal that she is 'in love' with Catherine's brother James. It becomes a little like a conversation between Mrs Allen and Mrs Thorpe, each woman's conversation limited to her own obsession.

First, Isabella brings up Catherine's confessed attraction to Henry Tilney in order to prompt Catherine to ask her about her own attachment. That fails, and Catherine, far from playing the distraught heroine, remains sensibly aware she may never see Tilney again, and changes the subject back to books. Isabella tries once more, returning the topic of conversation to men, and noting her personal preference for men with sallow complexions and light eyes. 'You must not betray me', Isabella begs, 'if you should ever meet with one of your acquaintance answering that description' (p. 41). Again, Catherine completely misses the point, and when Isabella asks her to drop the subject, frustratingly for her companion, takes her at her word. Notice how often Isabella attempts – and fails – to script a role for Catherine to play.

STUDY FOCUS: THE MARRIAGE MARKET | A04

Isabella is the prime shopper in *Northanger Abbey*, at least when it comes to husbands. Her active pursuit of the two young men at the end of this chapter is telling. First, by claiming to be taking Catherine to see her new hat, rather than pursuing the young men, she shows how she treats husbands and hats in a manner reminiscent of the narrator's more **ironic** and self-conscious mixing-up of 'pastry, millinery, [and] young men' (p. 43) in the following chapter. Second, and more importantly, Isabella, with nothing but her looks and her ambition to help her, struggles to position herself in the marriage market as the active shopper or at least as the seller and not as the goods. She aims to be the one who looks and who chooses, an active agent and not the object of the male gaze. In this respect, she is trying to change the rules of the game, a game in which, Henry Tilney later says, 'man has the advantage of choice, woman only the power of refusal' (p. 74). Should we, however, at least admire her efforts? What other options would a woman in her position have?

CONTEXT | A04

The 'male gaze' is a term popularised by film critic Laura Mulvey to describe the way women are objectified in film through the audience being placed in the perspective of the heterosexual man.

CONTEXT | A04

'Genteel' women in Austen's England could not work, unless they became governesses. They were financially dependent upon men and upon making a good marriage, a point underlying the ironic opening of *Pride and Prejudice*: 'It is a truth universally acknowledged that a single man in possession of a good fortune must be in want of a wife.'

EXTENDED COMMENTARY

VOLUME ONE, CHAPTER 6, PP. 38–40

In this passage, the **narrator ironically** offers us a conversation between Catherine and Isabella to demonstrate their mutual affection, and the 'delicacy, discretion, originality of thought, and literary taste which marked the reasonableness of that attachment' (p. 38). It is, however, also very much a passage about reading and readers. For the first time, **Gothic** fiction becomes directly central, and it functions in two main ways. First, it establishes some of the plot devices and **tropes** that will influence Catherine's imagination and expectations when she goes to Northanger Abbey in Volume Two. Second, it helps to illuminate the very different characters of Catherine and Isabella.

While Gothic fiction is usually considered to originate with Horace Walpole's *Castle of Otranto* (1764), it is Ann Radcliffe, the focus of Catherine's interest here, who had the most influence on the development of the **genre** in the late eighteenth century and early nineteenth century. Catherine is reading *The Mysteries of Udolpho* (1794), with its typical Radcliffean emphasis on a threatened and suffering heroine, imprisonment and male tyranny. In this, the most famous of Radcliffe's novels, the orphaned Emily St Aubert is carried off by her aunt's villainous husband Montoni to the remote castle of Udolpho in the Apennines. He is after her fortune rather than her honour, but Emily believes both, and her life, to be threatened. Many of the terrors to which she is subjected appear to be supernatural, but are later explained away as the product of natural and human causes. The novel continues on for many more chapters after Emily escapes Udolpho, until, after enduring further trials, she is finally reunited with her true love Valancourt.

Catherine has just got to the lifting of the black veil. This black veil is a central device for creating suspense and terror in the novel. Emily approaches it with trepidation, but when she finally gains the courage to lift it, she sees something that frightens her so much that she drops senseless on the floor. The reader is then left in suspense for hundreds of pages before it is finally revealed that Emily thought she saw a mouldering corpse. However, if she had looked more closely she would have seen that it was only a wax statue, a *memento mori*: that is, a representation and reminder of death and not death itself.

CONTEXT **A04**

The 'explained supernatural' is characteristic of Radcliffean Gothic **romance** while the kind of Gothic horror associated with Matthew Lewis, author of *The Monk* (1796), exploits 'real' demons and ghosts.

CHECK THE FILM **A03**

In Andrew Davies's 2007 film adaptation of *Northanger Abbey*, Catherine reads and is thrilled by not just Ann Radcliffe's *The Mysteries of Udolpho* but also Matthew Lewis's highly risqué *The Monk*, a book Austen links to John Thorpe. Catherine's fantasies change accordingly, and have clear sexual overtones that are missing in Austen's novel.

Emily proves herself a superficial reader in failing to see that the body behind the veil is only a wax statue, and in this respect the mystery of the black veil plays into Austen's similar concerns with reading: reading books and reading people. Catherine is also a superficial reader and must learn to be more discerning. This is made particularly clear in this passage by the way she takes everything Isabella says or does at face value. She does not recognise that someone might say one thing and mean or do another. She does not distinguish illusion from reality, surfaces from depths. While this shows Catherine to be naive, it also establishes her as pleasingly honest and forthright in contrast to Isabella.

In *The Mysteries of Udolpho*, Radcliffe's main interest is actually not in what lies behind the veil but in the veil itself: in the role that the veils – or the masks and disguises we assume – play in constructing our identities. We might say the same of Austen in *Northanger Abbey*: it is certainly this aspect of the veil that relates to the characterisation of Isabella. Isabella is also a superficial reader, but in a quite different way. Indeed, we might be justified in wondering if she ever actually reads a book or if she simply uses literature as part of her self-display. She professes knowledge of fashionable literature as part of the formation of her stylish personality. Isabella clearly has not read the so-called 'Northanger canon' that she has listed in her pocketbook. She knows they are all 'horrid' (p. 39), that is, they are frightening, because 'a particular friend of mine, a Miss Andrews, a sweet girl, one of the sweetest creatures in the world, has read every one of them' (p. 39). Samuel Richardson's *Sir Charles Grandison* (1754), on the other hand, Isabella declares 'an amazing horrid book' (p. 40), with horrid now being used to mean bad, because the same Miss Andrews 'could not get through the first volume' (p. 40). Isabella consequently assumes it is not readable. Finding herself in a difficult position since Catherine – who has read and enjoyed Richardson's novel – knows more than her, Isabella, who always wants to be in control, quickly changes the subject to headdresses.

As her treatment of Miss Andrews well demonstrates, Isabella's idea of friendship is similarly superficial. She clearly does not think Miss Andrews is beautiful, quite the reverse, but she finds her very useful in the games she plays with men. Making them say Miss Andrews is beautiful before she agrees to dance with them, Isabella implies she is making them lie, as she no doubt is, and draws attention to her own beauty in contrast. She is indeed 'incapable of real friendship' (p. 39). Immediately after claiming she would never stand to hear anyone speak slightingly of her dear friend Catherine, she calls her dear friend Miss Andrews 'insipid' (p. 40). Isabella views friends, like everything else, as something to be used to her own advantage. How, we should now be wondering, is she using Catherine? Why is she determined to be dressed exactly like Catherine that evening? Catherine, still an undiscerning reader of others, is quite oblivious to being manipulated by Isabella.

Language also functions to reveal character in this passage. Isabella is, to begin with, imprecise in her use of words, as her use of 'horrid' well shows. Isabella's language is also overly dramatic and exaggerated; like a sentimental heroine of romance, she professes her feelings too often and too vehemently. Something is not just horrid, but 'amazing' horrid (p. 40); she does not just wait, but waits for 'ten ages' (p. 38). Catherine is always the 'dear' or 'dearest creature' (pp. 38, 39, 40), while Miss Andrews is always the 'sweetest' (p. 39). There is certainly, to return to the narrator's introductory comment, nothing 'reasonable' about her conversation or language. Catherine's language is beginning to reveal Isabella's influence. When speaking of *The Mysteries of Udolpho*, for example, she enthuses very much in the exaggerated style of her supposed friend: 'I should like to spend my whole life in reading it' (p. 39).

Isabella's influence on Catherine will, however, soon be checked by her growing friendship with the Tilneys, and it would be useful to read the exchange here in light of Henry Tilney's later lecture to Catherine on her indiscriminate use of 'nice' and the very different discussion of Gothic fictions to be found in Volume One, Chapter 14.

CONTEXT **A04**

The other Gothic books listed in Isabella's pocketbook have come to be known as the 'Northanger canon'. They were initially thought to be the product of Austen's imagination. By 1927, however, the bibliographer and critic Michael Sadleir had proven the existence of all the novels and renewed critical interest in Gothic fiction.

VOLUME ONE, CHAPTER 7

SUMMARY

- Catherine and Isabella encounter their brothers, James Morland and John Thorpe.
- John insists he will take Catherine for a drive the next day and engages her to dance that evening.
- Catherine attempts to discuss novels with John.
- James is clearly infatuated with Isabella but Catherine does not see this.

ANALYSIS

JOHN THORPE

John Thorpe is simultaneously the most objectionable and the most comic character in the novel: a buffoon and a bore. As in the case of his sister, language is important in demonstrating his character. He is, as James observes, 'a little of a rattle' (p. 49): that is, John 'rattles' on about nothing of much consequence. So, of course, do his mother and sister. John's conversation, or rather (and the **narrator** is insistent on this distinction in the next chapter) his 'talk' (p. 64) with Catherine is full of loud boasting about horses, carriages, hunting, card games and other topics that would be of little interest to her.

Compare him in this respect with Henry Tilney who, as his conversations with Mrs Allen on muslins (see p. 28) and with Catherine on novels (see pp. 102–4) demonstrate, is able to discuss topics of interest to his female companions – and even if he sometimes amuses himself at their expense. Conversation as opposed to talk, Henry demonstrates, is an exchange, and something that enlarges upon and develops a topic. John's talk, full of contradictions, goes nowhere. His profane bluster, rather than making him sound like a man of the world, only emphasises his vulgarity. Furthermore, he is a liar; here his dishonesty is limited to relatively trivial matters, such as his exaggerated claims about the abilities of his horse. Later, however, his lies will have much more harmful consequences for Catherine.

CRITICAL VIEWPOINT A03

Some critics read John Thorpe as the true villain of *Northanger Abbey*. Others consider he is as incapable of filling the role of villain as Catherine is of filling the role of sentimental heroine. As you read through the novel, consider which position you find the most convincing.

CHECK THE BOOK A04

Matthew Lewis's *The Monk* (1796) was the subject of **parody** in R. S.'s *The New Monk* (1798) in which the corrupt monk lusts not after the body of the virginal young heroine who turns out to be his sister, as in the original, but instead after her money ... and a juicy leg of pork.

STUDY FOCUS: A 'RATTLE' ON READING   A01

Once again Austen draws on reading habits as a means of characterisation. John Thorpe is initially simply dismissive about novels, claiming that he has better ways to spend his time. He has apparently, however, read Henry Fielding's *Tom Jones* (1749), a novel notorious for the sexual adventures of its hero, and Matthew Lewis's *The Monk* (1796), a **Gothic** horror novel full of sexual exploitation, rape, incest and murder, and his choices make an implicit comment on his character.

John is clearly unfamiliar with Radcliffe's *The Mysteries of Udolpho* (1794), despite his attempted bluffing, and in this respect again compare him with Henry Tilney, who finishes it in two days, his 'hair standing on end the whole time' (p. 103). And John misunderstands and is dismissive of *Camilla* (1796), one of Austen's favourite novels, and shows himself a bigot when he says of the author Frances Burney (Madame d'Arblay) that 'as soon as I heard she had married an emigrant, I was sure I should never be able to get through it' (p. 48).

M.G. LEWIS.

THE LANGUAGE OF CARRIAGES

Few of Austen's characters, who are usually members of the middle or upper-middle classes, travel by public transport, that is, by stagecoach or hackney coach, the equivalent of a bus today. Private carriages, however, were expensive commodities and heavily taxed.

John Thorpe is introduced to us through his carriage and his erratic driving: he drives along 'with all the vehemence that could most fitly endanger the lives of himself, his companion, and his horse' (p. 43). His relatively cheap, cheerful and sporty gig, a carriage with two wheels and one horse, is bought second hand, and indirectly compared with Tilney's curricle, which has two horses and is much more elegant and expensive. Modes of transport will play a particularly significant role when Catherine goes to, and is then ejected from, Northanger Abbey.

STUDY FOCUS: MILSOM STREET — A04

Location is always important in Jane Austen's works, and it is worth finding out a little about the significance of some of the areas of Bath that she mentions. Milsom-street, for example, was an affluent and fashionable neighbourhood in the new part of Bath, and it is significant that the Tilneys lodge here. Milsom-street was also, however, already developing its reputation as an exclusive shopping mall, full of the imposing bow-fronted shop windows that appeared towards the end of the eighteenth century. It is here that Isabella has seen in one of those shop windows the hat with coquelicot – a brilliant and fashionably new shade of orange-red – ribbons. When the narrator observes, then, that 'though they overtook and passed the two offending young men in Milsom-street, [Isabella] was so far from seeking to attract their notice, that she looked back at them only three times' (p. 46), this is more than an **ironic** dig at Isabella. The location is as important as anything else in this sentence. In this world of affluence, and of tempting shop windows, Isabella is established as both commodity – she wants them to look at her – and purchaser. She is at the same time the one who looks, and who looks for something that will bring her both wealth and status. See also **Part Three: Themes**, on **Consumer culture**.

GLOSSARY

44	**devoirs**	an act or expression of respect or courtesy

KEY QUOTATION: VOLUME ONE, CHAPTER 7 — A01

John Thorpe: 'Novels are all so full of nonsense and stuff; there has not been a tolerably decent one come out since Tom Jones, except the Monk ...' (p. 47).

Possible interpretations:

- In light of Austen's defence of the novel, Thorpe damns himself with this generalisation.
- Plays with the word 'decent' to make an ironic comment on Thorpe's character: there is much that could be considered 'indecent' in both books.
- Imprecise and slangy language ('and stuff') sets Thorpe in opposition to the precision of Henry Tilney.

CONTEXT — A04

Carriages were markers of degrees of wealth and status. At the bottom of the scale are those like James Morland who, as we find out in the next chapter, has to hire a carriage because he cannot afford his own. Closer to the top of the scale is General Tilney who has a fashionable and expensive chaise-and-four, an ostentatious display of wealth (p. 148).

CONTEXT — A04

In *The Cambridge Companion to Jane Austen*, ed. Copeland and McMaster (2011), Juliet McMaster suggests how Austen marks degrees of wealth for the middle class: 'Number of servants marks incomes at lower levels; the acquisition of a carriage does it for incomes that are a bit higher; and the "house in town" certifies the presence of great incomes' (p. 134).

VOLUME ONE, CHAPTER 8

SUMMARY

- At the ball that evening, John Thorpe immediately goes to the card room.
- Henry Tilney asks Catherine to dance but, engaged to dance with John, she is forced to refuse.
- Catherine meets Henry's sister Eleanor.
- Isabella and James Morland are preoccupied with each other all evening and Catherine is left on her own.

ANALYSIS

FRIENDSHIP

The chapter starts with Austen encouraging the reader to consider the nature of true friendship. Isabella, upon meeting Catherine, is full of smiles and affection, and admires both her gown and her hair. But how genuine is this behaviour? Described by the **narrator** as 'the usual ceremonial' (p. 51) what should be impulsive and warm is placed within the straightjacket of ritual. Then, after protesting with her usual exaggeration that 'not for all the world' (p. 51) will she dance with James and leave Catherine alone, three minutes later Isabella does precisely that. The reader has certainly seen through Isabella by now, even if Catherine has not. Her protestations of friendship are as false as everything else about her. Isabella is an arch dissembler, that is, someone who assumes false appearances.

Catherine's first meeting with Eleanor suggests a quite different relationship. They go through 'the first rudiments of an acquaintance' (p. 55), but it goes no further that evening. Contrast this with her very first meeting with Isabella in Chapter 4. There, Isabella and Catherine talk on all those subjects which, the narrator **satirically** observes, have much to do with 'perfecting a sudden intimacy between two young ladies: such as dress, balls, flirtations, and quizzes' (p. 32). The affection and attachment of the two girls is immediate, a convention of **romantic** novels. But true intimacy, Austen suggests, is not achieved suddenly but develops over time, as will Catherine's friendship with Eleanor.

STUDY FOCUS: STYLE AND ELEGANCE A02

Be alert to other contrasts that are made between Isabella and Eleanor in terms of appearance and manner, and consider what they might signify. The former, for example, has 'resolute stillishness' while the latter 'more real elegance' (p. 54). Language here is telling. If elegance, the word always associated with Eleanor, has connotations of grace, taste and timelessness, stylishness is modish: of the moment, caught up in current fashions. There is an underlying class issue here, with Eleanor, of the gentry, having 'good breeding' on her side (p. 54), and Isabella, of not quite the same social stature, in contrast being somewhat vulgar. And there is also an underlying financial issue. Isabella has to make do with cheap ribbons or bits of lace to make a dress look new; there are no inherited pearls for her, as, we will soon discover, there are for Eleanor. The contrast is typical of the way Austen tends to divide her characters into the landed gentry and the urban mercantile or professional classes, old money and new money.

THE EYE OF THE WORLD

Eleanor is described as being able to be 'young, attractive, and at a ball, without wanting to fix the attention of every man near her' (p. 54). This is another **ironic** comment on that consummate social performer, Isabella, who wants precisely this attention, and part of a larger concern with vision in this chapter. So much of life, even courtship, in Jane Austen's fictional world is carried on and monitored under the public gaze, in the ever-vigilant 'eye of the world' (p. 52). And this is particularly true in the ballroom, where the two main activities are dancing and watching. Remember the first ball when Catherine and Mrs Allen attempt to gain a 'comprehensive view' (p. 22) of the company below. In the public eye, any infraction, any inappropriate display, will be noticed. This is something that Isabella might court, but Catherine, as the parody of sentimental romances here well demonstrates, seeks to avoid.

STUDY FOCUS: PARODIES OF THE ROMANCE   A03

Austen is by no means the first to parody the sentimental romance or its heroine. The difference, however, is that Austen's heroine is most unlike the stereotype being parodied. In most other parodies the heroine does attempt to act as though she is living a romance novel. The first of these is Charlotte Lennox's *The Female Quixote* (1752), whose heroine Arabella is addicted to French romances and expects her life to be similarly adventurous. She even throws herself into the Thames at one point to escape horsemen she assumes are intent on 'ravishing' her.

This is also the approach Austen took in her **juvenilia**, such as *Love and Freindship* (sic), written when she was fourteen. In *Northanger Abbey*, however, her approach is different. Catherine has no illusions about herself and makes no attempt to play the sentimental heroine. Instead Austen parodies the romances through an ironic reporting of just how *unlike* their heroines Catherine is – how very much more sensible. When John goes to the card-room he leaves Catherine humiliated, appearing to have no dancing partner but, in line with social conventions regulating behaviour, she is unable to accept another offer as she is engaged to him. The narrator appropriates the exaggerated language of sentimental novels to describe Catherine being 'disgraced in the eye of the world' (p. 52) even though John's rudeness is really the 'source of her debasement' (p. 52). The language is, of course, more appropriate to a heroine who has lost her honour than a girl abandoned by her dancing partner.

This is typical of Austen's strategy in parodying the sentimental romance: she invokes a convention only to deflate it. Catherine may suffer, but only for ten minutes. Similarly, Catherine sensibly assumes the lady on Henry's arm is his sister, rather than his wife, and consequently, rather than turning deathly pale and 'falling in a fit on Mrs. Allen's bosom' (p. 52), Catherine stays 'in the perfect use of her senses' (p. 52).

VOLUME ONE, CHAPTER 9

SUMMARY

- The next day, Catherine plans to go to the Pump-room in the hope of meeting Eleanor Tilney again.
- James, Isabella and John arrive, with the intention of taking her on a drive to Claverton Down.
- Catherine reluctantly agrees, and endures a tedious ride with John during which he insinuates she will be heir to the Allens' fortune.
- On return, Catherine learns that Mrs Allen had met Henry and Eleanor while out walking and she regrets the missed opportunity to meet them.
- Catherine learns that Mrs Tilney died a while ago.

ANALYSIS

MATTERS OF JUDGEMENT

When pressed to join John for a drive in his gig, Catherine appeals to Mrs Allen for advice about whether or not she should go. Mrs Allen is quite wrong in telling Catherine, 'with the most placid indifference' (p. 60), to do as she pleases. During this time, a young unmarried woman should not be alone with a man; she should be accompanied by a chaperone.

Mrs Allen's judgement, the **narrator** stresses at the end of this chapter, is not to be trusted in any matters. As Catherine questions her about the Tilney family, Mrs Allen is generally vague about whether Mrs Tilney is dead or alive. It is typical of her obsession with dress and possessions that she does, however, remember that the previous Miss Drummond's father, upon her marriage, gave her £20,000 (which would of course immediately become her husband's) and 'five hundred to buy wedding-clothes' (p. 67). Notice how precise her memory is when it comes to such matters. Similarly, she remembers the beautiful pearl necklace Eleanor inherited from her mother. This settles the issue: Eleanor has inherited the necklace so Mrs Tilney must be dead. When Catherine asks her if Mr Tilney is the only son (which would mean he would inherit) do we assume that she has similarly material concerns in mind or is this simply not part of Catherine's character?

STUDY FOCUS: THE TRAVELLING HEROINE **A02**

In Jane Austen's time, improvements in roads and in carriage design led to an increasing amount of travel for pleasure. Travelling is prevalent in all Austen's novels: each features at least one, and usually many, trips. *Northanger Abbey* is particularly full of journeys. There are three main journeys which structure the novel – between Fullerton and Bath, Bath and Northanger Abbey, Northanger Abbey and Fullerton – but there are also numerous other shorter journeys such as the drive in this chapter. Each literal journey could be said to contribute in some way towards Catherine's most **metaphorical** journey: her development from child to adult.

In this particular journey, Catherine, who has not been 'in the habit of judging for herself' (p. 65), begins to have the courage to trust in her own opinions. Previously, flattery and friendship, along with James's declaration that John is just the kind of man that women like, have persuaded her to say that John is 'very agreeable' (p. 49). By the end of this trip, however, she will be able to 'resist such high authority' (p. 65). His duplicity, along with his obsession with himself and his own concerns, lead her to wonder whether he is indeed 'altogether completely agreeable' (p. 65).

CONTEXT **A03**

Miss Bingley in *Pride and Prejudice* (1813) also has a fortune of £20,000, which translates after investment to £1,000 a year. Such wealthy landowners as Mr Darcy have incomes of over £4,000 a year. For more information on money in Jane Austen, see Edward Copeland on 'Money' in *The Cambridge Companion to Jane Austen*, ed. Copeland and McMaster (2011).

CRITICAL VIEWPOINT **A03**

Ellen Moers, who coined the term 'female Gothic' in *Literary Women* (1976), characterises Ann Radcliffe's use of the **Gothic** as a feminine substitute for the **picaresque** that allowed her 'to send maidens on distant and exciting journeys without offending the proprieties' (p. 126).

VOLUME ONE, CHAPTER 10

SUMMARY

- The Allens, Thorpes and Morlands meet at the theatre that evening and Isabella continues to pursue James.

- The next day, Catherine goes to the Pump-room and meets Miss Tilney. During their conversation Catherine unintentionally reveals her feelings about Henry.

- Catherine considers what to wear the following evening at the cotillion ball where she will see the Tilneys again.

- Mr Tilney asks her to dance. John attempts to interrupt. Mr Tilney compares dancing to marriage.

- Catherine sees General Tilney talking to Eleanor, and Henry explains that it is his father.

- Henry and Eleanor propose they should all take a walk the following day, with the Tilneys to collect Catherine at noon.

ANALYSIS

LANGUAGE AND CONVENTIONS

The narrator's attack on Isabella's duplicity and self-absorption continues in this chapter, as comparisons are again made between Catherine's exchanges with Isabella and her exchanges with Eleanor. Both exchanges are, in different ways, conventional, it must be noted. Isabella's conversation is marked by the **hyperbole** and repetition typical of the sentimental **romance**, with such extravagances as 'I can hardly exist till I see him' (p. 68). Her exchange with Catherine takes place, importantly, within a theatre, and Isabella is calling upon the scripted roles of romance in a manner that simply bewilders her friend. Henry also drew on scripts during their first conversation, but he is playing with and **satirising** the social codes. Isabella wants her role-playing to be taken seriously.

When Isabella remarks on the discovery that her tastes and opinions are (supposedly) exactly those of James, for example, she expresses relief that Catherine was not there since 'I am sure you would have made some droll remark or other about it' (p. 69). Catherine simply does not understand the role Isabella wants her to perform: 'Indeed you do me injustice; I would not have made so improper a remark on any account' (p. 69). Eleanor and Catherine have a subsequent conversation that is also marked by convention, but social conventions. They say nothing that has not been said before, and so their conversation is also scripted, but the difference is that they speak 'with simplicity and truth, and without personal conceit' (p. 70).

Catherine always responds in an honest and forthright manner. She still seems unaware of the point of Isabella's numerous hints in this chapter, but now finds them improper. When talking with Eleanor she is equally forthright, although she does not intend to be or realise what she has revealed about her feelings for Henry.

> **CRITICAL VIEWPOINT** **A02**
>
> In *Jane Austen in Context*, ed. Janet Todd (2005), Anthony Mandal notes that Isabella Thorpe is one of Austen's characters who uses 'language as a social tool, employing the contemporary discourse of sensibility to hide their mercenary natures and grasping ambitions' (p. 25).

CHECK THE BOOK A04

For a discussion of propriety, see Jane Nardin, *Those Elegant Decorums: The Concept of Propriety in Jane Austen's Novels* (1973).

STUDY FOCUS: PROPRIETY   A04

In Austen's time, an elaborate code of etiquette governed genteel social life, and this meant a certain standardisation of behaviour. In *Jane Austen and the Fiction of Culture* (1999), Richard Handler and Daniel Segal explain that this is because 'etiquette is used to represent and establish social status' (p. 91). Knowing how to behave in a certain way represents your affiliation with a certain class. So when the **narrator** remarks that the conversation between Catherine and Eleanor was conventional, with not an expression or an observation being made that had not been made repeatedly every Bath season, we need to recognise the serious point beneath the **irony**. Catherine's ability to engage properly in this social exchange is one indication that she would be a suitable partner for Henry Tilney, despite the fact that he is socially superior to her.

Austen's characters 'constantly scrutinize others' use of communicative codes in order to assess their claims to relative social status' (see Handler and Segal, p. 91). And so, as readers, should we. In this chapter, both Isabella and John give themselves away in terms of social status through vulgar discussion or behaviour. When John talks to Catherine while she is dancing with Henry, why is Henry so annoyed? Given his usual manner of speaking, one can imagine Henry's ironic tone when he repeats the word 'gentleman' to describe John.

CHECK THE BOOK A04

For more information on dancing and dances of the time, see Cheryl A. Wilson, *Literature and Dance in Nineteenth-century Britain: Jane Austen to the New Woman* (2009).

DANCING

Before about 1800, an evening of dancing at public assemblies such as those in the Lower or Upper Rooms at Bath would begin with about an hour of minuets. The minuet was a dance for only two persons at a time. This was very much a public performance, done under the eyes of hundreds of spectators. Those who wished to dance applied to the master of ceremonies who ordered partners appropriately, with consideration given to rank.

In Austen's time, however, the lively and, importantly, more *social* English country-dances had come to be preferred to such stately and complicated French dances such as the minuet. Most country-dances were performed in a so-called 'longways' set for five to eight couples, with partners standing across from each other. The dance began with couple one at the top dancing first with couples two and three, and then with couples three and four, and so on. While waiting for their turn during the dance, couples were able to talk, and this explains how Catherine and Henry can have such an extended conversation during the dance. Dances are important in Austen's novels, partly because of the opportunities they provide for courtship. In *Jane Austen and the Province of Womanhood* (1989), Alison Sulloway notes that 'with the exception of Anne Elliot [in *Persuasion*], all the heroines either meet their lovers at balls or their creator provides them with a crucial scene at a ball' (p. 155).

STUDY FOCUS: DANCE AND MARRIAGE   A04

The characters of whom Jane Austen most approves are always those who can comment upon and analyse social conventions at the same time as they participate in them. Henry, for example, does precisely that here when he develops an elaborate **metaphor** with dance as an emblem of marriage.

Henry is playful in his comparison, but there are serious underlying points. Dancing in this society offers the chance to play at and explore being a couple, without the finality of matrimony. This is made quite clear by considering exactly who takes part in the dancing. Only women who were 'out', that is, presented to society, took part in dancing, and if women no longer danced (like Anne Elliott in *Persuasion* who instead plays the piano for others to dance) this tended to signal they were past marriage and had moved into spinsterhood. Married couples could dance, but rarely did, although, particularly at private balls, married men were expected to help when unattached women lacked partners. Those who danced, as a result, tended to be only the men and women eligible for marriage.

CONTEXT   A04

The thirty-seven-year-old Jane Austen comments on growing older: 'By the bye, as I must leave off being young, I find many Douceurs [much compensation] in being a sort of Chaperon for I am put on the Sofa near the Fire & can drink as much wine as I like' (letter to sister Cassandra, 6 November 1813).

GLOSSARY

69   **his glass of water** the supposedly health-giving waters from a natural spring; up to 8 litres would be drunk per day

71   **cotillion** a dance in which four couples change partners while moving through a series of set figures

71   **tamboured** tambour work was done with the muslin stretched on a frame; it involved using a hook like a tiny crochet hook to pierce the fabric and make a design with a chain stitch

71   **the mull or the jackonet** both are high-quality muslins, very soft, thin and transparent

KEY QUOTATION: VOLUME ONE, CHAPTER 10   A01

Henry Tilney: 'man has the advantage of choice, woman only the power of refusal' (p. 74).

Possible interpretations:

● An **aphorism** suggesting one of the ways in which dancing is like marriage.

● Suggests the limitations on and expectations of women in the late eighteenth century.

● Henry's statement may not be entirely true, as the next chapter demonstrates.

REVISION FOCUS: TASK 1   A04

How far do you agree with the following statement?

● In the world of *Northanger Abbey*, conventions are essential to the ordering and regulation of society.

Try writing an opening paragraph for an essay based on this discussion point. Set out your argument clearly.

VOLUME ONE, CHAPTER 11

SUMMARY

- The next morning it rains until half past twelve. The Tilneys do not appear.
- Isabella, John and James arrive in two open carriages insisting they are all to go on a drive.
- John claims he has seen Henry and Eleanor driving up Lansdown road and that he heard Henry say they were going to Wick Rocks.
- Catherine, tempted by the chance of seeing Blaise Castle, consequently agrees to accompany them.
- They see the Tilneys on their way to pick up Catherine, and it becomes clear John has lied.
- They have left Bath too late so they turn back without seeing the Castle.

ANALYSIS

MONEY MATTERS

This chapter shows Catherine's attitudes towards the Thorpes beginning to change. The Thorpes may have temporarily succeeded in keeping Catherine away from the Tilneys, but this triumph will not last long. Catherine is no longer even concerned to attempt being agreeable to John, and Isabella's self-absorption means she has little interest in consoling Catherine – and this is something Catherine, finally, notices.

And just in case the reader had not yet realised the reason for the Thorpes' pursuit of the Morlands, it becomes quite clear in this chapter. John's references to the miserliness of 'people who rolled in money' (p. 85), prompted by James not having his own carriage, suggests he thinks the Morlands to be wealthier than they are, and Catherine destined to inherit the Allens' wealth.

More indirectly, Isabella is said to find consolation for not reaching Clifton in 'a pool of commerce, in the fate of which she shared, by private partnership with Morland' (p. 86). Commerce is a gambling card game which begins with all players contributing to a common pool. But commerce also indicates the nature of Isabella's interests, and what she really wants to share, with James.

GRADE BOOSTER **A02**

Examiners want to see you paying close attention to the language and analysing specifics, not just making large general statements. With Isabella in particular, this involves attention to the language of commodities and the market, such as the seemingly innocent reference to a card game here, which just happens to be called 'commerce'.

STUDY FOCUS: THE POWER OF REFUSAL? **A03**

Following on from Henry's claim in the previous chapter that women have only the power of refusal, this chapter questions whether women possess even such limited power. While Catherine is consoling herself with fantasies of Blaise Castle (spelled Blaize by Austen) as a kind of Udolpho, she is actually experiencing an updated version of a classic **Gothic** abduction scene. As a number of critics have pointed out, *Northanger Abbey* duplicates many of the conventions it **parodies** and this is one good example. Catherine is persuaded into John's carriage under false pretences, and then, when it becomes clear that he lied, he refuses to stop and she is basically his prisoner. Furthermore, he appears to relish his power over her: he 'only laughed, smacked his whip, encouraged his horse, made odd noises, and drove on' (p. 84). Those 'odd noises' are particularly disturbing; he seems to be deriving a little too much pleasure from this abduction. Catherine, with no 'power', no ability to get away, is forced to 'submit' (p. 84). In this particular scene, at any rate, she has no power of refusal.

CRITICAL VIEWPOINT **A04**

Northanger Abbey comments upon and parodies the Gothic novel. At the same time, as in this 'abduction', it domesticates and enacts many conventional Gothic **tropes**, placing the action within the world of middle-class English society.

EIGHTEENTH-CENTURY FOLLY

Blaise (or Blaize as Austen spells it) Castle is on the north-western outskirts of Bristol. It is not, as John Thorpe tells Catherine, the oldest castle in England but simply a miniature castle, a picturesque folly built in 1766 by Thomas Farr, a Bristol merchant whose wealth was built on sugar plantations and the slave trade. A folly can be very simply defined as an architectural construction that is not what it appears to be. Follies have no function apart from decoration and they are purpose built as mock towers, temples, castles, ruins and even pyramids.

Blaise Castle, then, as Austen and most of her readers knew, is a fake. This serves two functions. First, although Catherine never realises the truth about the castle, readers aware it is a folly will see how this anticipates Catherine's false expectations and subsequent disappointment with Northanger Abbey. Second, Austen comments on the characters of the Thorpes by associating them with this rather unnatural and somewhat vulgar aspect of the **picturesque**: the folly is a garden feature that is the predecessor, one might say, of our modern garden gnomes. Consider how Austen here uses setting to comment upon her characters by comparing the association of the Thorpes with the picturesque with the way Eleanor and Henry are linked to the picturesque in Volume One, Chapter 14.

> **CRITICAL VIEWPOINT** A03
>
> In *The Cambridge Companion to Jane Austen*, ed. E. Copeland and J. McMaster (2011), Thomas Keymer notes, 'Even as Catherine's spine tingles at the thought of Blaise Castle, Austen evokes dungeons built on the suffering not of medieval serfs but of modern slaves' (p. 30). Austen develops this issue further in *Mansfield Park* (1814), where the luxuries of Sir Thomas Bertram's estate are similarly built on the exploitation of slaves.

STUDY FOCUS: GOTHIC VISIONS   A03

Early critics complained about the structure of the novel, claiming the social comedy of the Bath volume had little to do with the **Gothic parody** of the second, but many would now contest this point. Certainly, the language of the Gothic begins to creep into this chapter as Catherine anticipates seeing a real-life Udolpho. She is torn between thoughts of Gothic pleasures to come and the pleasures of being with the Tilneys that she has missed. In Austen's memorable phrasing, she thinks 'by turns, on broken promises and broken arches, phaetons and false hangings, Tilneys and trap-doors' (p. 83). The ludicrousness of the mix is emphasised by the **alliteration**, but there is a serious point here too. Catherine is repeatedly encountering deception and false promises; Bath is a confusing world she cannot understand. She thinks too that she would give up all the pleasures of Blaise Castle if only the Tilneys did not think ill of her. However, the rather long and detailed list of these pleasures as she anticipates her progress through a long series of lofty rooms (p. 84) suggests that her enthusiasm has not been completely dampened. There is perhaps some **irony** in the fact that true Gothic heroines usually end up being taken to a ruined Gothic pile when they are abducted. For this updated abducted heroine, being taken to a ruined Gothic pile is her only source of comfort.

> **CRITICAL VIEWPOINT** A03
>
> Emily Brontë's *Wuthering Heights* (1847) has also sometimes been considered a structurally hybrid form, with the novel split into the first-generation plot, the Gothic story, and the second-generation plot, a rewriting of the first as domestic realism.

GLOSSARY

80	**St. Aubin**	St Aubert, father of Emily, heroine of Radcliffe's *The Mysteries of Udolpho* (1794)
82	**phaeton**	a highly fashionable four-wheeled open carriage

VOLUME ONE, CHAPTER 12

SUMMARY

- Catherine calls on Eleanor to explain what happened the previous day.
- She is turned away, although it is clear Eleanor is at home.
- At the theatre that evening, Henry comes to their box. Catherine explains.
- Plans are made for the projected walk to take place soon.
- Catherine observes John Thorpe speaking with General Tilney, and perceives that she is the subject of their conversation.
- John tells Catherine that the General admires her.

CRITICAL VIEWPOINT A03

In 'John Thorpe, Villain Ordinaire: The Modern Montoni/Schedoni', Nancy Yee argues John is the true villain of the novel and suggests how Austen aligns him with Radcliffe's villains Montoni and Schedoni, from *The Mysteries of Udolpho* (1794) and *The Italian* (1797) respectively. See *Persuasions On-Line*, 31.1 (Winter 2010). This journal is easily accessible online to all.

ANALYSIS

PLOTTERS AND PLOTTING

This chapter concludes with a sentence that, certainly in retrospect, takes on a touch of **irony**: 'The evening had done more, much more, for her, than could have been expected' (p. 92). Catherine is thinking that it has been a good evening because she is reconciled with Henry and Eleanor and, in addition, it appears General Tilney, whom she assumed disliked her, actually admires her. But, unknown to her, the evening has also seen the initiation of the plot that will lead to her **Gothic** adventures in Volume Two. The reader is perhaps a little more suspicious about the huddled exchange between John and the General, and rightly so. The General's supposed admiration, as we later learn, is purely the product of John Thorpe exaggerating Catherine's wealth.

STUDY FOCUS: THE LAWS OF WORLDLY POLITENESS   A04

Elaborate codes of conduct governed all aspect of social life in Jane Austen's time. Social calls were regulated by a strict set of conventions, and the calling card was an essential part of visiting. One would pass one's card to a servant who would then take it to the master/mistress of the house. An unaccompanied woman would never call on a gentleman, of course, which is why Catherine goes to visit Eleanor, not Henry. It was considered bad form to say one was not at home when one actually was, and so Catherine is right here to assume she has been snubbed, even if it turns out to be at the prompting of General Tilney and not Eleanor.

Henry is more polite than his father, but at the theatre that evening he knows how to make his displeasure known, simply through the type of bow he gives Catherine: 'such a bow! no smile, no continued observance attended it' (p. 88). He believes that they were snubbed by Catherine on the previous day. Catherine, however, is far less tied to social conventions. He speaks with reserve and 'calm politeness' (p. 89), but she quite wildly pours out her explanations, with little restraint; she is described as 'thoroughly artless' (p. 90), making a clear contrast between her and the always artful Isabella. It is Catherine's openness and honesty that seem to captivate Henry.

GLOSSARY

91   **chair** a sedan chair, enclosed and on poles, carried by porters

VOLUME ONE, CHAPTER 13

SUMMARY

- Isabella, John and James decide to go to Clifton on the following day.
- Catherine, engaged to walk with the Tilneys, refuses to accompany them.
- John slips away and tells Eleanor that Catherine has to put off the walk.
- Catherine, enraged, goes directly to the Tilneys' house to explain.
- Catherine is introduced to General Tilney: he is very polite and welcoming.
- Mr Allen pronounces on the impropriety of Catherine's previous excursion with John, Isabella and James.

ANALYSIS

WHAT IS RIGHT AND WHAT IS PROPER

Austen's female **protagonists** frequently have to make their way in the world without the guidance of responsible parents or guardians. Consider, for example, the problematic parenting of the Bennets in *Pride and Prejudice* (1814), Sir Walter Elliot in *Persuasion* (1818) and Mr Woodhouse in *Emma* (1815). In *Northanger Abbey*, Catherine is separated from her parents and her guardian proves completely inadequate. The lack of moral or social guidance she receives is emphasised in this chapter by the constant use of words such as 'right', 'wrong', 'proper' and 'propriety'. While Mr Allen confirms the impropriety of young men and women driving around the country together and going into inns and other public places, this is something he should have done before.

Mrs Allen now agrees it is objectionable – but only because open carriages are 'nasty things' (p. 99): one gets splashed and one's clothing gets dirty. Then, when pushed by her husband and forced to consider matters of propriety, she excuses herself by turning the blame on to Catherine: 'Young people do not like to be always thwarted' (p. 100) she says, and uses the incident in which Catherine ignored her advice and bought a sprigged muslin. Catherine objects that this is a minor issue and the breach of propriety in accompanying John and Isabella was a matter of 'real consequence' (p. 100) but, unlike Catherine, Mrs Allen is unable to make such fine distinctions.

STUDY FOCUS: PERFORMANCE **A02**

Isabella's behaviour in this chapter, as she attempts to get Catherine to come to Clifton with them, is a calculated performance in a three-part structure. First, she attempts affectionate cajoling, and is full of flattery and endearments. When that fails, she moves on to pretending to be hurt, suggesting Catherine is dropping her 'best and oldest friends' (p. 94) – remember they have known each other for less than a week – for strangers, and finally resorting to tears in order to ensure James becomes part of the act. When Catherine continues to refuse, she moves into 'cold resentment' (p. 95) and James takes over: 'you were not used to be so hard to persuade' (p. 95). Once again we see just how compromised women can be in terms of that power of refusal.

VOLUME ONE, CHAPTER 14

SUMMARY

- Catherine and the Tilneys walk around Beechen Cliff.
- They discuss Radcliffe's *The Mysteries of Udolpho,* history and language.
- Henry instructs Catherine in the **picturesque**.
- Catherine comments on a 'shocking' thing to come out of London (p. 107) and Eleanor misunderstands her.
- Eleanor invites Catherine to dinner in two days' time.

CHECK THE BOOK **A04**

Jane Austen wrote her own *History of England* at fifteen, a **parody** of the standard schoolroom histories of the time and illustrated by her sister Cassandra. Exposing conventional biases, Austen placed Mary Queen of Scots at the centre of English history.

ANALYSIS

THE TORMENT OF HISTORY

In the defence of the novel offered in Volume One, Chapter 5, the **narrator** notes how history is set against novels in a literary marketplace that values the former and devalues the latter. This is once again an issue here, with Catherine's preference for novels set against Eleanor's fondness for history. Catherine finds history a 'torment' (p. 105). She reads it as a 'duty' (p. 104), but it both vexes and wearies her. In particular she points to the gender bias of history: 'the men all so good for nothing, and hardly any women at all' (p. 104). Novels, of course, particularly the **Gothic romances** that Catherine reads, centre on the adventures of female characters.

This is a moment which has been the focus of much critical debate. It seems dangerous to conflate Austen with the naive Catherine, or to see Catherine at any time as her mouthpiece. Nevertheless, the novel overall could be said to point to the pedagogical value of novels over history, since it is Catherine's reading of Mrs Radcliffe that leads to her desire to uncover the buried history of Mrs Tilney in Volume Two. Whether this is a good or bad thing, of course, is something you will need to decide.

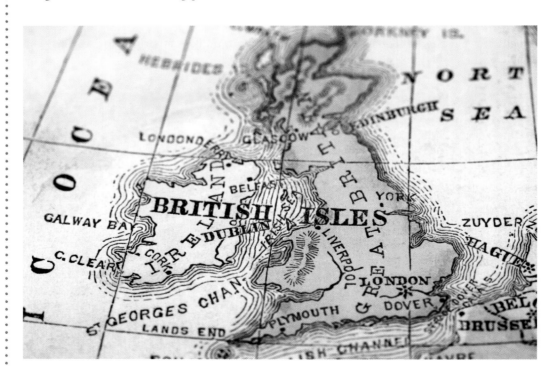

STUDY FOCUS: LOOSE WITH LANGUAGE — A02

One of Austen's preoccupations throughout her novels is the possible misuse of language. When Catherine calls *The Mysteries of Udolpho* 'the nicest book in the world' (p. 103), for example, Henry objects to what he sees as the banal use of the word. Catherine uses it to mean something that is agreeable, that gives pleasure. Henry, following Samuel Johnson and his dictionary – the most authoritative dictionary of the late eighteenth and nineteenth centuries – limits the word to mean what is accurate and precise. Henry similarly objects to Catherine's use of 'amazingly', a word suggesting the influences of both Isabella and the Gothic novel. What Henry is showing Catherine here is the need for discrimination, something that must be a part of one's use of language as well as one's assessment of people. Do you think then, as it is sometimes suggested, that Henry becomes Austen's mouthpiece here, or do you think, like Eleanor, that he is being too pedantic, 'more nice than wise' (p. 104).

CRITICAL VIEWPOINT A04

For Claudia Johnson in *Jane Austen: Women, Politics and the Novel* (1988), Henry Tilney is as much a bully as John Thorpe, even if his bullying is more polished. 'A self-proclaimed expert on matters feminine, from epistolary style to muslin, Tilney simply believes that he knows women's minds better than they do' (p. 37).

KEY QUOTATIONS: VOLUME ONE, CHAPTER 14 — A01

Henry on novels: 'The person, be it gentleman or lady, who has not pleasure in a good novel, must be intolerably stupid' (p. 102).

Henry on the understanding of women: 'In my opinion, nature has given them so much, that they never find it necessary to use more than half' (p. 109).

Catherine's thoughts on Henry: 'It was no effort to Catherine to believe that Henry Tilney could never be wrong' (p. 109).

GLOSSARY

103	**to stay**	to wait
103	**your friend Emily**	the heroine of Radcliffe's *The Mysteries of Udolpho*

EXTENDED COMMENTARY

VOLUME ONE, CHAPTER 14, PP. 106–8

Most critics agree that Catherine has to learn something in the course of the novel, but what that is, and who teaches her, have been matters of debate. Some critics believe Catherine educates herself through her own observations; others consider that Henry is both Austen's mouthpiece, sharing her **irony**, and Catherine's teacher, and that he teaches her such things as how to act in society, how to read and how to play with convention. While this passage indeed establishes Henry as her mentor, it also demonstrates some limitations to his beliefs and values.

We first see this in the discussion of the **picturesque**, an important aesthetic category in Austen's world. The Tilneys and Catherine have taken a day trip to Beechen Cliff, a popular site with tourists at the time. The rise of tourism took place between 1770 and 1830, which is also the age of the classic **Gothic** novel, and tourism and the Gothic share some similar interests, specifically the past, architecture and the picturesque. Austen was thoroughly familiar with William Gilpin's writings on the picturesque, and his ideas form important context for this passage. Picturesque beauty, Gilpin wrote, is associated with 'undressed simplicity' and 'native beauty' in Nature, 'that kind of beauty which would look well in a picture. Neither grounds laid out by art, nor improved by agriculture, are of this kind' (*Observations on Western Parts of England*, 1798, p. 328). An interest in the picturesque arose precisely when such landscapes were being lost, when the agrarian revolution was dividing up the land, when common ground was lost as land was enclosed by hedgerows and became the sole property of the rich and influential.

For the Tilneys, the walk around Beechen Cliff offers a chance to indulge their taste in the highly fashionable picturesque. While this on one level establishes them as people of taste and education, on another it may suggest some limitations. When Catherine earlier in the chapter observes that she can never look upon Beechen Cliff without thinking of the south of France, Henry is surprised to think she has been abroad. Of course, she has not. This is offered to us as a humorous moment: she is actually viewing the landscape through the Gothic writings of Ann Radcliffe. But when the Tilneys discuss the landscape, they view and assess it, through the writings of Gilpin, according to 'its capability of being formed into pictures' (p. 106). Perhaps they are equally guilty of viewing the world through some kind of filter, some artificial lens? We might even wonder, when Catherine initially puzzles over the idea that a clear blue sky is no longer to be taken as proof of a fine day, if her simple perspective might serve on some level to expose the fashionable discourse of the Tilneys as to some degree an affectation.

Henry also makes a number of rather condescending comments on the understanding of women in this passage, and although Eleanor begs Catherine to pay no attention, claiming that he is being playful and not serious, we might wonder whether this is the case. The **narrator** notes that Catherine is unaware of the advantages of ignorance, and does not know that an attractive, affectionate and ignorant girl (one in need of teaching,

CHECK THE BOOK **A04**

Stephen Copley's *The Politics of the Picturesque* (1994) is a collection of essays with some references to Austen, including an excellent essay by Ann Bermingham entitled 'The Picturesque and Ready-to-wear Femininity'.

that is), 'cannot fail of attracting a clever young man' (p. 106). It is probably not really Catherine's lack of knowledge that is being **satirised** here. Rather it is Henry's pleasure in being able to display his intellectual prowess.

Henry concludes his lecture on the picturesque by eventually moving to government and politics, and from there to silence. Catherine breaks this silence by saying, in a solemn tone, 'I have heard that something very shocking indeed, will soon come out in London' (p. 107). Since Henry has just given his commentary on the 'state of the nation' (p. 107), it is not surprising that Eleanor immediately assumes that Catherine is speaking of impending violence and riot. Of course, Catherine is thinking of books. Gothic **romance** becomes conflated with revolution: literary terrors become literal terrors. For Henry, this is simply amusing, another example of the misuse of language, with 'expected horrors' (p. 108) being the main offending phrase this time. The conflation, however, must be read in the context of the time, when concerns were raised about the moral and political influences of Gothic fiction and when the excesses of Gothic did become associated for many with the violent excesses of the French Revolution.

Following the French Revolution and the fall of the Bastille in 1789 – and during the time Austen was writing her first draft of *Northanger Abbey* (1798–9) – there was a widespread fear that similar social revolution might occur at home, and England during the period from 1794 to the end of the century saw numerous repressive measures, such as the Seditious Meetings Act and the Treasonable Practices Act, being passed in order to maintain order. It is no wonder, then, that the confused Eleanor is sure that the government will take 'proper measures' (p. 107) to prevent the riots.

Henry laughs at the confusion of the two women; satirising his 'stupid sister', he says, 'the riot is only in your brain' (p. 108). To Catherine he explains that instead of thinking of a new publication, Eleanor has been envisioning riots, with 'the Bank attacked, the Tower threatened, the streets of London flowing in blood' (p. 108). His satire implies that life in England is far more orderly than that, but in fact what he describes does not emphasise the absurdity of Eleanor's assumption. Quite the contrary, since what he describes resembles some of the disturbances that had already created chaos in the capitol in recent years, including the Gordon Riots of 1780, anti-Catholic riots that raged over a week in London, with 12,000 troops deployed to quell the uprising, and over 700 people killed. Something dreadful *has* come out of London, in precisely the manner Eleanor assumed.

To what extent, then, do we consider that Henry Tilney is, as some critics have argued, the mouthpiece of Jane Austen and the wise teacher of Catherine? The position that the reader decides to take on Henry in this chapter will have important implications for how he is seen in Volume Two. Is he the voice of reason and authority, or a man over-confident in his opinions?

CHECK THE BOOK **A03**

Victor Frankenstein's abandoned creature, spreading havoc and terror in Mary Shelley's *Frankenstein* (1818), has also been connected with the French Revolution.

CONTEXT **A04**

Exemplifying the connection made between revolution and Gothic, one essay in *The Monthly Review* magazine in 1793, entitled 'The Terrorist System of Novel Writing', warns that Gothic romances have established a 'SYSTEM OF TERROR, if not in our streets, and in our fields, at least in our circulating libraries, and in our closets.'

CRITICAL VIEWPOINT **A04**

Some critics have argued that the subsequent course of the novel shows, as Claudia Johnson puts it in *Jane Austen: Women, Politics and the Novel* (1988), 'that the misunderstanding between Catherine and Eleanor is plausible and even insightful: political unrest and gothic fiction are well served by a common vocabulary of "horror" because they are both unruly responses to repression' (p. 39).

REVISION FOCUS: TASK 2 — A02

How far do you agree with the following statement?

● Henry Tilney, as his sister says, is more 'nice' (particular) than wise in his attitude to language.

Try writing an opening paragraph for an essay based on this discussion point. Set out your argument clearly.

VOLUME ONE, CHAPTER 15

SUMMARY

- Isabella sends a note asking Catherine to visit as soon as she can.
- Isabella tells her she is engaged to James and he is about to ask for his father's consent to their marriage.
- The letter giving consent arrives, and Isabella begins imagining her future.
- John clumsily tries to propose marriage to Catherine.

ANALYSIS

SENTIMENTAL HEROINE

The capacity to feel strongly is the primary characteristic of the sentimental heroine. Isabella, who is repeatedly insisting that her attachments are strong, speaks here of the sleepless nights she has had, of growing 'wretchedly thin' (p. 113), and of her complete disregard for money: 'Where people are really attached, poverty itself is wealth' (p. 114) she claims. It is no wonder that Catherine finds her friend reminds her of 'all the heroines of her acquaintance' (p. 114). Isabella is throwing herself completely into the role. But if Catherine were wiser, she would see how Isabella repeatedly undermines her own views. Isabella's recollection that she lost her heart the moment she saw James, for example, is immediately followed by her remembering that she wore her yellow gown with her hair up in braids. Demonstrating her complete self-absorption, the only real details that she recalls from that moment are to do with herself and her appearance; the other descriptions, as Catherine recognises, could have been drawn from any sentimental **romance**. Sentimentalism, Austen suggests, is a pose drawn from books and not nature.

STUDY FOCUS: CONSUMERS A01

Complementing Isabella's self-absorption, the chapter focuses on the Thorpe family's concern with material possessions. Things in Austen's novels both add to the realistic details and take on **symbolic** qualities. Consider how this works with Maria's account of the previous day's outing to Clifton, where all they appear to do is consume goods of various kinds. They drove directly to a hotel and 'ate some soup' and arranged for an early dinner, went to the Pump-room and 'tasted' the water, bought souvenirs, ate ices and then quickly 'swallowed' their dinner before returning home (p. 111). They are indeed consumers. It is also interesting to observe that they do absolutely nothing they could not have done by staying in Bath – they do not even consider going to Blaise Castle – and the excursion to Bristol is thus set in contrast to the excursion to Beechen Cliff in the previous chapter.

MATERIAL GIRL

Despite her protestations than money does not signify and that her 'wishes are so moderate' that 'the smallest income' would suffice (p. 114), what Isabella envisions is a life of some luxury. 'A cottage in some retired village' becomes a villa around Richmond, a suburb of London, and, then as now, a very affluent neighbourhood (p. 114). We are rarely given access to her mind – what she is really thinking is perhaps clear enough without that – but here we are made privy to Isabella's musings as she imagines her future as the wife of James. Notice in particular the emphasis on visual display when she imagines herself 'the *gaze* and admiration' of all new and old friends: 'a carriage at her command, a new name on her tickets [her visiting cards], and a brilliant *exhibition* of hoop rings on her fingers' (p. 116, emphasis added). The plain gold wedding band that signifies marriage has been replaced by something designed to make quite another statement.

STUDY FOCUS: PLAYING WITH JOHN? **A02**

John, in his usual blustery and half-incomprehensible manner, tries to suggest (without actually ever proposing) marriage to Catherine. In previous encounters with John, Catherine has been at a loss; here she plays the game of manners beautifully and, intentionally or not, manages to hold him at bay. Jane Nardin, in *Those Elegant Decorums* (1973), has noted in reference to Austen's *Sense and Sensibility* (1811) that propriety is necessary in a social whirl constituted by selfish, stupid or vulgar people (pp. 24–5), and this is shown beautifully in this passage from *Northanger Abbey*. John is fended off by politeness. But does Catherine actually understand the game here? Is she just acting as though she has no idea what he really means when she assures him most politely that he will always be welcome at Fullerton, that her parents will be very glad to see him, and she will too, since 'Company is always cheerful' (p. 118). Catherine exploits polite behaviour in order to manage this conversation, but does she really have any idea what he is really saying?

GLOSSARY

| 111 | **spars** mineral fragments that would be used as souvenirs |
| 113 | **sarsenet** a soft fine silk |

VOLUME TWO, CHAPTER 1

SUMMARY

- Catherine dines with the Tilneys. She finds her friends restrained and feels uneasy with the General but is unsure why.
- The next evening Catherine meets Henry and Eleanor and their brother at the ball.
- Catherine dances and talks with Henry. Isabella dances with Captain Tilney.
- James's second letter arrives, explaining the intentions of Mr Morland with regard to income.
- Isabella is clearly disappointed in the amount.

ANALYSIS

THE MYSTERY BEGINS

In Volume One, the reader is generally distanced from Catherine and shares the **narrator**'s superior understanding of people and events. While Catherine is duped by Isabella, for example, the narrator's arch and **ironic** comments ensure we are not. In Volume Two, Austen's strategy changes. There is a mystery here. Why are Henry and Eleanor so restrained when Catherine visits, what is the tension between them and their father, and why does Catherine feel that although the General is attentive and charming, she does not enjoy his company and it is 'a release to get away from him' (p. 123)? As Catherine puzzles over this, so does the reader. We can guess that the problem lies with him, but the nature of the problem still remains a puzzle. From now on we are encouraged to share more in Catherine's errors, and the mystery will be fully revealed to us only when it is revealed to Catherine.

CHECK THE BOOK A03

Catherine is not the only Austen heroine to be duped, but usually when this happens, as in the case of Willoughby and Marianne in *Sense and Sensibility*, Wickham and Elizabeth in *Pride and Prejudice* or Frank and Emma in *Emma*, the reader is, from the start, duped too.

CONTEXT A03

The title for *Northanger Abbey* was chosen by Austen's brother and sister after her death. Between 1784 and 1818 more than thirty novels appeared with 'Abbey' in the title, and many more with words like 'Convent', 'Monk', 'Priory' or 'Nun'. Some readers may therefore have been surprised to find this was not formulaic Gothic fiction.

STUDY FOCUS: ENTER CAPTAIN TILNEY A03

The handsome Captain Tilney shows no inclination to admire Catherine, and so the narrator ironically declares her safe from him in terms appropriated from **romance**: '*He cannot be the instigator of the three villains in horsemen's great coats, by whom she will hereafter be forced into a travelling-chaise and four*' (p. 125). This reminds us that Catherine has previously been 'abducted' by John Thorpe, although in a much less impressive gig, and it also **foreshadows** her trip to Northanger Abbey in a chaise-and-four (p. 148). Furthermore, while Captain Tilney is no **Gothic** tyrant, he will turn out to be a villain of kinds, as will his father the General. Both Captain and General Tilney consequently provide good examples of how, at the same time as Austen **parodies** Gothic conventions in Volume Two, she enacts them in an updated and domestic context, bringing horror home to contemporary England. What warnings do we have in this chapter that the Captain is going to be trouble? What does Henry suggest when he says that the Captain dancing with Isabella is 'no more than I believed him perfectly equal to' (p. 127)?

'INCONSTANCY IS MY AVERSION'

While Isabella is urging Catherine to forget the supposedly unworthy Henry, she claims that 'inconstancy is my aversion' (p. 124). However, when she immediately agrees to go to the ball, but decisively states that she will not dance when it is quite clear she plans to, she begins to reveal her own inconstancy. Isabella is always saying one thing and doing precisely the opposite. Dancing with Captain Tilney, who is the heir to the Tilney fortune, may at this point simply be a way of basking in his admiration and the envy of others. 'I saw every eye was upon us' (p. 128), she says to Catherine, and note here the stress on the visual again: Isabella is not just watched, she is watching herself being watched.

FORTUNE HUNTING

When the letter from James arrives, Isabella's dissatisfaction is quite clear. This is a setback: £400 a year is by no means what she had anticipated, and we can almost hear the cogs turning in her mind as she begins plotting her next move. She is obviously not going to be content with an income she dismisses as 'hardly enough to find one in the common necessaries of life' (p. 129). Recognising Catherine is hurt, Isabella quickly tries to recoup her position, claiming her dissatisfaction is with having to wait two years. When her mother says 'we perfectly see into your heart. You have no disguise' (p. 130), the irony is that we do, and Mrs Thorpe, despite her best efforts, does not.

CONTEXT **A04**

Four hundred pounds a year in Austen's time is an income that could support genteel life, but not easily. It would allow for at least a cook and a housemaid but certainly no carriage. See Edward Copeland on 'Money' in *The Jane Austen Companion*, ed. Copeland and McMaster (2011) for more information about the standard of living associated with various incomes.

STUDY FOCUS: SPEAKING WELL ENOUGH TO BE UNINTELLIGIBLE — **A02**

'I cannot speak well enough to be unintelligible' (p. 126), Catherine tells Henry in an unintentional but brilliant piece of **satire**. Perhaps it is not just a satire on modern language generally, however, as Henry sees it, but also a comment on his own ironic conversation. Catherine certainly often finds him quite unintelligible. Notice how even within this particular exchange, she has to query his meaning repeatedly: 'What do you mean?', 'I do not understand you' and 'pray tell me what you mean' (p. 126). Does Henry sometimes speak so 'well' he becomes unintelligible?

GLOSSARY

127 **hands across** a move in country dancing

REVISION FOCUS: TASK 3 — **A03**

How far do you agree with the statement below?

- Catherine Morland is an odd heroine for an Austen novel since she is of limited understanding and even occasionally 'stupid'.

Try writing an opening paragraph for an essay based on this discussion point. Set out your argument clearly.

VOLUME TWO, CHAPTER 2

SUMMARY

- The General decides that the Tilneys will leave Bath.
- Catherine is invited to stay with the Tilneys at their home in Gloucestershire.
- Catherine's imagination, fed with **Gothic romance**, is excited by the idea of visiting Northanger Abbey.

ANALYSIS

HISTORICAL NORTHANGER

As Eleanor tells Catherine at the close of this chapter, Northanger Abbey had fallen into the hands of an ancestor of the Tilneys upon the Dissolution of the Monasteries by Henry VIII (1536–40). Its origins as a private estate, therefore, are based in that part of history in which Catherine is particularly uninterested: the 'quarrels of popes and kings' (p. 104).

STUDY FOCUS: GOTHIC NORTHANGER · A03

Catherine, as we already know, has little interest in being 'tormented' by history. Anticipating her visit to Northanger, 'so active were her thoughts' (p. 134) that she does not seem to pay much attention to the historical explanation Eleanor provides. Catherine views Northanger not through the lens of history but through the lens of the Gothic. Her imagination immediately supplies her with details about what she might expect: long, damp passages, narrow cells, ruined chapel and, with luck, 'some awful memorials of an injured and ill-fated nun' (p. 134). The use of the **free indirect style** begins to increase, with the narration beginning to reflect her excited expectations. These expectations are soon to collide with the realities she will encounter.

Where the historic and the Gothic versions of Northanger meet is in their anti-Catholicism. As Henry VIII set himself in opposition to the Catholic Church, so Gothic of the late eighteenth century set up enlightened and rational Protestant England in direct opposition to what it constructs as a feudal, superstitious and barbaric Catholic Europe. (See **Gothic**, in **Part Four: Form**.) It is this that produces the common Gothic **trope** of the nun walled up alive. Historically, prior to the Dissolution, this abbey was a 'richly-endowed convent' (p. 134), suggesting a site of female independence. Gothic, however, tends to depict convents as sites of oppression for women. You should keep this in mind in considering Catherine's later Gothic imaginings. Does Northanger Abbey become a Gothic space of female oppression under the rule of General Tilney?

VOLUME TWO, CHAPTER 3

SUMMARY

- After not seeing Isabella for a few days, Catherine meets her in the Pump-room.
- Isabella tells Catherine that John loves her and thinks she has encouraged him. Catherine is astounded.
- Captain Tilney appears and he and Isabella flirt in front of Catherine.

ANALYSIS

A NEW SCHEME AFOOT

This chapter focuses on the developing relationship between Isabella and Captain Tilney. Their intimacy is revealed to the reader as soon as Isabella familiarly calls him 'Tilney'. Isabella only began to call James 'Morland' instead of 'Mr Morland' after the announcement of their engagement (p. 113). This completely bypasses Catherine, as does the significance of Isabella's response when Catherine says that even if she does not marry John, she and Isabella will still be sisters. '"Yes, yes," (with a blush) "there are more ways than one of our being sisters.—But where am I wandering to?"' (p. 137). We certainly understand where Isabella's mind is 'wandering to'. She is thinking that Catherine will marry Henry and that there is the possibility she may marry Captain Tilney.

STUDY FOCUS: 'WE HAVE EYES' `A02`

The language of the visual, of seeing and being seen, pervades this chapter. Isabella seats herself on a bench that offers a good place both to see and be seen while claiming 'it is so out of the way' (p. 135). This is typical of the double-speak associated with her. Repeatedly she says one thing and means quite another; language for her is a means of attempting to disguise her real intentions. She is, of course, sitting there in anticipation of the arrival of Captain Tilney.

Isabella reminds Catherine of her supposedly 'foolish trick' of 'fixing' her eyes on something when she is thinking (p. 135): following Henry's 'niceness' about language, we might suggest 'scheming' would be the more correct choice of word. As soon as she sees Captain Tilney enter, Isabella, 'fixing her eye on him', catches his notice (p. 138). The word 'fix' here suggests Isabella wants to catch and secure him as a husband.

All Isabella has to bargain with is her beauty, and this Tilney appreciates: 'we have eyes; and they give us torment enough' (p. 139). This is a relatively steamy exchange and shows Austen not as unaware of sexual matters as some critics have argued in the past. Tilney looks at and enjoys Isabella's body; his flirting pushes the boundaries of propriety. Compare this with the more intellectually playful courtship of Henry: he talks to Catherine much like he talks to his sister. Indeed, in admiring the 'elasticity' of her walk (p. 98), General Tilney shows more awareness of Catherine's physical attractions than does Henry.

VOLUME TWO, CHAPTER 4

SUMMARY

- Catherine is increasingly disturbed by the relationship between Captain Tilney and Isabella.
- She asks Henry to intervene. He says his brother is already aware of Isabella's engagement and there is nothing he can do.
- His brother will soon leave Bath, he tells her, and the flirtation will end.
- Catherine allows herself to be reassured.

ANALYSIS

DOUBLE STANDARDS?

Why is it that in this chapter Henry initially seems reluctant to enlighten Catherine as to what is actually going on? While Isabella is thinking in terms of marriage, it is already clear Captain Tilney is not. Catherine questions Henry persistently about his brother's behaviour, and his reticence implies he is in a difficult situation; he can hardly say to the naive Catherine that his brother is something of a rake.

There is also the sense, however, that Henry believes Isabella is really to blame, and he appears to downplay what his brother is doing: 'No man is offended by another man's admiration of the woman he loves; it is the woman only who can make it a torment' (p. 143). Henry's double standards in terms of gender are, of course, characteristic of his society, and so it is harder to take him to task for them – although Eleanor does. He describes his brother as 'a lively, and perhaps sometimes a thoughtless young man' (p. 143) in something of a 'boys will be boys' manner. As his aside that the officers in the regiment 'will drink Isabella Thorpe for a fortnight' (p. 144) suggests, however, her reputation could be seriously compromised.

STUDY FOCUS: EDUCATING CATHERINE

The idea that **pedagogy** is an essential element to love in Austen's novels has a long history: Austen frequently writes about misguided girls being educated and corrected by wiser and often older men with whom they fall in love. Juliet McMaster writes in *Jane Austen and Love* (1978) that 'the pedagogic relationship is not parasitic but symbiotic, a relationship that is mutual and joyful: it blesseth him that gives, and him that takes' (p. 45). Others, however, argue that many readers exaggerate the tutor-like function of Austen's leading men, or fail to consider that if they do educate the women they marry, they also need to learn a lot themselves Do you agree? Does Henry have something to learn too?

CHECK THE FILM A03

In Andrew Davies's 2007 film adaptation, Eleanor extends some pity to Isabella: 'Your friend', Davies's Eleanor tells Catherine, 'has dealt with your brother very badly, but I fear she is out of her depths with mine.'

CHECK THE BOOK A03

The connection between pedagogy and love is considered from very different perspectives in the perverse relationship between the **narrator** and the marquis in Angela Carter's 'The Bloody Chamber' (1979) and in the relationship between Catherine and Hareton in Emily Brontë's *Wuthering Heights* (1847).

VOLUME TWO, CHAPTER 5

SUMMARY

- The journey to Northanger Abbey begins. Catherine accompanies Eleanor in the chaise-and-four.
- The General suggests Catherine move into the curricle with Henry.
- Henry teases Catherine with a sensational **Gothic** tale of what will happen to her at Northanger.
- The abbey, once she arrives, is light and modern, and nothing like what Catherine had imagined.

ANALYSIS

THE TRAVELLING HEROINE

Once again, carriages become a means of suggesting personality. The General's fashionable chaise-and-four in which Eleanor and Catherine ride is a luxurious carriage designed to impress. Everything is excessive in terms of display, and at the same time everything is precise and ordered, reflecting the General's controlling hand: the postilions 'rising so regularly' and the 'numerous out-riders properly mounted' (p. 148). In spite of its grandeur, the chaise-and-four is 'heavy and troublesome' (p. 148), like the General himself, and Catherine much prefers Henry's curricle, with its light and nimble horses. The curricle ride also functions to move on the plot: it begins with Catherine's admiration of Henry's appearance and his skilful handling of the horses and ends with Henry's Gothic send-up, forming the transitional moment from courtship plot to Gothic tale.

STUDY FOCUS: HENRY'S GOTHIC TALE A02

Prompted by Catherine's assumption that Northanger will be 'a fine old place, just like what one reads about' (p. 149), Henry amuses her with a story about what will happen based precisely on such reading, making her the central **protagonist**. His **parody** of the mechanics of the Gothic primarily draws upon, and displays his knowledge of, incidents from three of Radcliffe's novels: *The Mysteries of Udolpho* (1794), *A Sicilian Romance* (1790) and *The Romance of the Forest* (1791). Henry beautifully mimics the language of the Gothic with such phrases as '*unconquerable* horror' (p. 150), 'fainting spirits' (p. 150) and 'the wretched Matilda' (p. 152). And he draws upon numerous familiar Gothic **tropes**, including sliding panels, mysterious portraits, subterranean passages, secret hiding places and found manuscripts. The highly conventional nature of the tropes and plot twists he appropriates is neatly suggested by his heroine's dismissal of drops of blood, daggers and signs of torture as 'nothing ... out of the common way' (p. 151), and he makes fun of the improbable nature of Gothic plots with his heroine's ability to open doors 'only secured by massy bars and a padlock' (p. 151).

Catherine almost seems to forget she is listening to a fictional story, something that the narrator of the novel we are reading – that is, *Northanger Abbey* – is always careful to remind us of. Keep Henry's tale in mind while reading the following chapters, and consider to what extent he is responsible for exciting Catherine's imagination. Does he, particularly through making her the female protagonist of his tale, encourage her to think of herself as a heroine in a Gothic adventure? Is it purely coincidence that there is a chest and a cabinet of ebony and gold in his story?

CHECK THE BOOK A04

For an accessible introduction to Gothic from its origins in the mid-eighteenth century to contemporary manifestations in the early twenty-first century, see Sue Chaplin's *Gothic Literature* (2011).

CHECK THE BOOK A03

'Silent, lonely and sublime, it seemed to stand the sovereign of the scene, and to frown defiance on all who dared to invade its solitary reign. As the twilight deepened, its features became more awful in obscurity, and Emily continued to gaze, till its clustering towers were alone seen, rising over the tops of the wood ... ' (Ann Radcliffe's description of the castle in *The Mysteries of Udolpho*, Vol. 2, Chapter 5).

A MODERN ABBEY

History is treated in two main ways in *Northanger Abbey*. On the one hand, we have imitations, as in the eighteenth-century folly Blaise Castle, which excites Catherine's imagination but which she never sees. On the other hand, we have improved and updated history, as Catherine finds on her arrival at Northanger, much to her puzzlement and disappointment. The language that is used to describe Northanger in the last part of this chapter aligns it not with the **Gothic**, but rather with the **Enlightenment** world, which, in defining itself in terms of light, rationality, order and modernity, constructed and defined the Gothic world in opposition as dark, superstitious, chaotic and primitive. (See also **Part Four: Form**, on **Gothic**.)

Northanger is described generally as modern and elegant. The fireplace, rather than being the massive and elaborately carved product of former times, is of the most up-to-date and efficient variety possible, and made of plain slabs of marble. Staircases are broad and made of shining oak, not winding, narrow and constructed of uneven stone. The windows are clear and full of light, suggesting openness rather than secrecy. They are Gothic in name, having the pointed arch that defines the Gothic window, but not in effect. All seems rational, clear and ordered, not least the General himself with his strict observance of punctuality. There would seem to be little opportunity for clandestine dark deeds here.

STUDY FOCUS: GOTHIC IMAGININGS A02

In showing Catherine to be first caught up in Henry's wild tale and then let down by the reality of Northanger, this chapter provides the first of what could be seen as four variations on one theme: Catherine getting caught up in Gothic imaginings only to be disillusioned and propelled back into the ordinary world. As you read on, try to identify which scenes fit this description, and see how her responses to the moment of disillusionment gradually change from puzzlement to embarrassment to shame.

STUDY FOCUS: A CLASSIC BILDUNGSROMAN   A03

The novel's emphasis on Catherine's education and her growth as a person makes it a classic **Bildungsroman**, and this has been a central concern of the critics from the start. Critics have always been divided, however, on the matter of how Catherine is taught and by whom and what she learns. Howard S. Babb, in *Jane Austen's Novels: The Fabric of Dialogue* (1962), sees Henry Tilney as Catherine's teacher. Stuart Tave, in *Some Words of Jane Austen* (1973), similarly claims that Catherine learns a moral art, and the values of common life from Henry.

GLOSSARY

148	**bait**	a stop to feed and water the horses
148	**postilions**	men who ride and guide the horses drawing a coach
148	**out-riders**	mounted attendants who ride in front of or beside a carriage
152	**scud of rain**	rain driven by the wind
153	**Rumford**	Benjamin Thompson, Count von Rumford: scientist and entrepreneur who devised efficient versions of such appliances as stoves and chimneys
153	**casements**	casement windows are hinged at the side, often containing glass panes held in place by strips of lead

KEY QUOTATION: VOLUME TWO, CHAPTER 5   A01

'To be sure, the pointed arch was preserved – the form of them was Gothic – they might be even casements – but every pane was so large, so clear, so light!' (p. 153).

Possible interpretations:

- Encapsulates Catherine's disappointment with finding a modernised abbey.
- Links Northanger with the Enlightenment values of reason and order.
- Suggests a need to be aware of the possible differences between appearance and reality.

CRITICAL VIEWPOINT   A03

Critics like Susan Morgan in 'Guessing for Ourselves in *Northanger Abbey*' (in *Jane Austen*, ed. Harold Bloom, 1986) see Catherine learning to make her own judgements and trusting her own instincts, rather than relying on Henry's lessons or sets of conventions.

VOLUME TWO, CHAPTER 6

SUMMARY

- Catherine discovers her room to be quite cheerful and comfortable.
- She sees an old heavy chest in a corner that sparks her curiosity, but Eleanor comes to get her for dinner and explains the presence of the chest.
- It is a stormy night. Preparing for bed, Catherine spots an old black cabinet resembling the one in Henry's story.
- She searches the cabinet and finds a roll of paper that she assumes is a secret manuscript. Her candle is extinguished and she cannot read it.
- She is frightened by the storm, distant footsteps and moans and cannot sleep until early in the morning.

CONTEXT **A04**

In the scene with the chest, there are echoes of the Greek myth concerning Pandora's box. Pandora was told never to open the box but, driven by insatiable curiosity, she opened it, releasing all the evil within into the world. She quickly shut it, but all that remained within was the spirit of Hope. To open Pandora's box has come to mean a small action with momentous consequences.

ANALYSIS

THE REAPPEARANCE OF THE CHEST

While Catherine finds her room to be reassuringly normal, and nothing like the room Henry described, it is not long before her imagination starts transforming the ordinary into the mysterious. Henry, one suspects, had exactly this 'immense heavy chest' (p. 155) in mind when telling his tale and including the detail of the 'ponderous chest which no efforts can open' (p. 150). Notice how Catherine immediately lets her imagination run wild. Austen **parodies** the **Gothic** as Catherine speculates that the broken handles on the chest were 'broken perhaps prematurely by some strange violence' (p. 156), and the initials engraved on the chest she describes as 'a mysterious cypher' (p. 156). When she finally opens the chest, however, it contains no skeletons, no memoirs of an ill-fated nun, but simply a 'white cotton counterpane, properly folded' (p. 156). Like the house itself, the bedspread, properly folded and innocently white, suggests the orderly and the ordinary. Why is Catherine no longer being guided by 'what was simple and probable' (p. 52) as when she sensibly assumes Eleanor is Henry's sister and not his wife. What has changed, we might ask, since then?

STUDY FOCUS: GOTHIC ADVENTURES WITH A CABINET

Despite the fact that Catherine is deeply ashamed of her 'absurd expectation' (p.157) with respect to the chest, the 'causeless fears of an idle fancy' (p. 159), it is not long before her imagination begins to work again. Consider some of the ways in which Catherine's searching in the cabinet duplicates the incident with the chest, in particular the sequence of emotions that move from apprehension to anticipation and to disappointment.

At first, the stormy night brings to mind numerous 'dreadful situations and horrid scenes' (p. 158), but Catherine, 'wisely fortifying' (p. 158) her mind, thinks of her own secure situation in *contrast* to these scenes. Such wisdom forsakes her, however, when she sees the cabinet. The cabinet is not exactly like the one in Henry's story but an imitation: ebony and gold are mimicked in the black lacquer and yellow paint – in other words it is a fake. Catherine recognises the similarity: 'though there could be nothing really in it, there was something whimsical, it was certainly a very remarkable coincidence!' (p. 159). The notion that there could be 'nothing really in it' could refer to either the connection with Henry's story or to the cabinet itself. It is surely no coincidence, however, as Henry no doubt planted the cabinet in his story in the knowledge Catherine would see this in her room.

BLUEBEARD

'The key was in the door, and she had a strange fancy to look into it' (p. 160). Female curiosity has been the focus of many moral tales since Pandora first looked into the box or Eve first tasted the apple. What is being referenced in this episode is not just the Gothic but also the epitome of all such tales of curious women: 'Bluebeard', a literary folktale by Charles Perrault. Bluebeard gives his wife a key to a small room, making her swear never to enter. When he is away, she gives in to curiosity and finds the floor of the room awash with blood and Bluebeard's former wives hanging from hooks on the walls. Catherine has the same transgressive desire to see and to know; her 'fearful curiosity' (p. 156) does not, however, lead to such horrific discoveries. The key is in this door because there is nothing within to hide; indeed, the door is not even locked.

CHECK THE BOOK A03

Angela Carter's 'The Bloody Chamber' (1979) offers one of many modern rewritings of the Bluebeard story. More generally, the idea of the forbidden room is central to much contemporary Gothic, most memorably rewritten perhaps in Stephen King's *The Shining* (1977), with Danny's curiosity about the ominous Room 237.

STUDY FOCUS: GOTHIC AND LANGUAGE A02

Henry's **parodic** tale can be seen as scripting Catherine's mock-**Gothic** encounter here, and this is emphasised not just by what happens but also by the language used in the two incidents. When asking if Catherine will be prepared for the horrors, Henry inquires with mock-seriousness, 'Have you a stout heart?' (p. 149), and here Catherine is described as entering her room 'with a tolerably stout heart' (p. 158). What other verbal connections can you find?

With the finding of the 'manuscript', the language increasingly echoes that of the Gothic. Catherine trembles and grows pale, 'her feelings at that moment were indescribable' (p. 161). This is a standard Gothic strategy, suggesting the inadequacy of language to capture inner experience (see also **Part Four: Language**). Simultaneously, there is a gradual movement from **omniscient narration** to **free indirect style**, so that the language increasingly becomes a reflection of Catherine's mind – 'The storm too abroad so dreadful!' (p. 161) – while the narrator is still detectable, commenting **ironically** on Catherine's experiences. Catherine's candle extinguished, she trembles as 'a sound like receding footsteps and the closing of a distant door struck on her affrighted ear. Human nature could support no more' (p. 161). The irony, of course, is that it is completely normal that there should be others walking around in the abbey, opening and closing doors.

CRITICAL VIEWPOINT A03

According to David Lodge in *The Art of Fiction* (1993), free indirect style 'renders thought as reported speech (in the third person, past tense) but keeps to the kind of vocabulary that is appropriate to the character, and deletes some of the tags, like "she thought" … that a more formal narrative style would require. This gives the illusion of intimate access to a character's mind, but without totally surrendering authorial participation in the discourse' (p. 43).

VOLUME TWO, CHAPTER 7

SUMMARY

- Upon awakening, Catherine immediately turns to the roll of paper and finds it to be nothing but a series of laundry lists.
- Henry has to go to Woodston for a few days on business.
- The General offers to show Catherine the house, but he decides to start with the garden.
- Eleanor shows Catherine her mother's favourite walk.
- Catherine questions Eleanor about Mrs Tilney and is soon convinced that the General must have been very cruel to her.

ANALYSIS

THE FOUND MANUSCRIPT

The convention of the found manuscript goes back as far as the first Gothic novel, *The Castle of Otranto* (1764). In the first edition, Walpole did not specify his authorship but rather had a fictitious editor claim in a preface that he found the manuscript in a library. Other Gothic novels that exploit this device are Radcliffe's *Gaston de Blondeville* (1826) and Sophia Lee's *The Recess* (1783–5). For Catherine, who is hoping to find hidden memorials of an ill-fated nun, or, as in Henry's story, something resembling the memoirs of the wretched Matilda, the discovery that it is simply a roll of washing bills is a moment of comic deflation. Once more her wild imaginings are replaced by shame as she recognises the 'absurdity of her recent fancies' (p. 164).

> **CHECK THE BOOK** **A03**
>
> Sue Chaplin has a helpful discussion of the found manuscript as exploited in *The Castle of Otranto*, *The Recess* and *Gaston de Blondeville* as well as other Gothic narrative strategies in her *Gothic Literature* (2011), pp. 181–205.

STUDY FOCUS: WASHING BILLS **A04**

There is, however, more to Catherine's discovery of the washing bills than a moment of comic deflation when the scene is considered from a gender perspective. The washing bills bring to the foreground things that are usually hidden in the **romance** novel. Sandra Gilbert and Susan Gubar, in *The Madwoman in the Attic* (1979), were among the first to argue that Austen here is pointing to the 'real threat' to women's happiness – a life of subservience and domesticity after marriage – in having Catherine find this list (p. 135). We must be careful, however, not to assume – as they imply – that a middle-class woman like Catherine might have had anything to do with washing in the late eighteenth century. Their reading is a little **anachronistic**. More convincingly, critics have recently suggested that the washing bill brings to light what Catherine seems not to recognise: the economic motivations that lie beneath the surface of the romantic courtship plot.

The washing bill incident also indirectly suggests how Austen is adapting the **genre** of the Gothic to the modern domestic world. When Catherine attempts to return the washing bills, she discovers that the chest that she had assumed locked was in fact always open. There is no need for the secret dark spaces associated with the Gothic here.

CONTEXT **A04**

Pineapples were first brought to England in 1657 and became the favoured novelty fruit in the eighteenth century. Called the 'king of fruits' or 'prince of vegetables', their cultivation required significant effort and expense.

CHECK THE BOOK **A03**

For a collection of essays on various aspects of the Gothic, including Antiquarianism, Parody, Architecture, Gothic Romance, the reading and publishing of Gothic texts, see Glennis Byron and Dale Townshend, eds, *The Gothic World* (2013).

THE GENERAL'S PINEAPPLES

From his breakfast set to his kitchen garden, the General shows that Northanger is just as much a world of commodities as Bath. And despite great differences in wealth, the General increasingly appears in other ways much like the Thorpes, as boastful as John and as concerned with self-display as Isabella. The primary examples of conspicuous consumption in this chapter are the village of hothouses (heated greenhouses) and the General's pinery. While the General claims the fruit is for family and friends, a sign of good nature and generosity, in fact it is produced primarily as a display of his wealth and importance.

STUDY FOCUS: THE GOTHIC VILLAIN A02

While Catherine is longing to see the house, the General insists on her first viewing the garden. As Eleanor is aware, but Catherine is not, it is his habit to walk in the garden at this time, and so this has nothing to do with the wishes of his guest. The General, as this tells us, is excessively controlling.

By the end of the chapter, however, Catherine has begun to suspect him of much more and is well on her way to envisioning him as a conventional **Gothic** villain. Catherine again starts to let her imagination get the better of her. How much justification is there for her assumptions about his having been an 'unkind husband' (p. 170)? Notice too how the language gets increasingly excessive. From describing him as 'unkind' Catherine moves to 'dreadfully cruel' (p. 171) and 'odious' (p. 171). Simultaneously, her own reactions to him become exaggerated. While she has previously expressed a feeling of oppression in his company, she now claims she felt 'terror and dislike' and that these have become 'absolute aversion' (p. 171). After the humiliating disappointments Catherine has experienced with the abbey, the chest and the cabinet, all of which have previously been worked upon by her Gothic imagination, does the reader already expect a similar moment of comic deflation with the General, or do we this time get caught up in her Gothic plot?

GLOSSARY

163	**breeches-ball** special soap used for cleaning men's breeches
169	**succession houses** a sequence of glass houses for forcing plants, differentially heated so that plants might be moved in succession through a regular gradation of climates

VOLUME TWO, CHAPTER 8

SUMMARY

- The General shows Catherine the house, but appears unwilling to show her the part of the house that looks most interesting.

- Eleanor tells her that part of the house contained her mother's room, the room in which she died. She promises to show the room to Catherine on another day.

- Catherine discovers Mrs Tilney died nine years ago, when Eleanor was not at home.

- Catherine begins to suspect the General and to wonder if Mrs Tilney still lives, imprisoned somewhere in Northanger.

ANALYSIS

SIZE MATTERS

One of the things that Austen has been repeatedly pointing out in the previous chapters is the General's competitiveness, and in particular his need to be assured that everything he has is not only better but bigger than what Mr Allen has. (He is, of course, assuming Catherine will inherit from the Allens.) This comes to a comic climax in this scene when the General shows Catherine the dining room and 'could not forego the pleasure of pacing out the length, for the more certain information of Miss Morland' (p. 173).

For Tony Tanner in *Jane Austen* (1986), the General embodies 'compulsive acquisitiveness' as 'a symptom of the new consumer urge of the age and the crass material instinct for competitive emulation it spawned' (p. 65). In *Women Writing about Money* (1995), on the other hand, Edward Copeland emphasises the General's snobbery, his attachment to a consumer culture in which things are valued not for what they are but rather for the prestige they confer (p. 92). Is the General primarily acquisitive or primarily a snob? What kind of a world does he – and Northanger – embody?

> **CRITICAL VIEWPOINT A03**
>
> Critics observe that Radcliffe's castle in *The Mysteries of Udolpho* (1794) is both the embodiment of Montoni and at the same time the embodiment of what Ian Duncan in *Modern Romance and Transformations of the Novel* (1992) calls 'decayed ancestral power': age, violence, tradition, law and **patriarchy** (p. 23).

CHECK THE BOOK A03

It is useful to compare Northanger Abbey with other more genuinely Gothic fictional houses, including Brontë's Thornfield Hall in *Jane Eyre* (1847) and Wilkie Collins's Blackwater Park in *The Woman in White* (1862). In both these buildings, women are indeed incarcerated.

STUDY FOCUS: THE AIR AND ATTITUDE OF A MONTONI A03

Catherine is not as concerned with the General's snobbishness or acquisitiveness as she is with her own 'blackest suspicions' (p. 176). As the General paces the drawing-room in the evening, she feels sure these are justified: the 'well-read' Catherine (p. 172) knows, 'It was the air and attitude of a Montoni!' (p. 176). Notice the **irony** when, soon after Catherine is described as 'well-read', she is shown the library and 'gathered all that she could from this storehouse of knowledge, by running over the titles of half a shelf' (p. 173).

Montoni is the villain of Ann Radcliffe's *The Mysteries of Udolpho* (1794). Although looking back in some ways to precursors in Jacobean drama, Montoni can be said to establish the prototype of the attractively cruel villain. After the heroine Emily's father dies, she is put in the care of his sister, Madame Cheron. The sinister Italian Montoni marries Emily's aunt, and takes her first to Venice, and then to his decaying castle, Udolpho, in the Apennines.

In a sense, Catherine's intuition here is spot on. However, she is distracted from the real issue by visions of Mrs Tilney being imprisoned and 'receiving from the pitiless hands of her husband a nightly supply of coarse food' (p. 177). This echoes the fate of Madame Cheron in *The Mysteries of Udolpho*, and Louisa Bernini in *The Sicilian Romance* (1790), kept a prisoner in her husband's castle and presumed dead by her children. What she should have remembered is that in spite of Emily's constant fears for her virtue in *The Mysteries of Udolpho*, what Montoni actually covets is her inheritance, not her body. General Tilney, as we might already suspect, is similarly motivated by financial concerns.

CHECK THE BOOK A04

Alistair Duckworth's *The Improvement of the Estate: A Study of Jane Austen's Novels* (1971) examines the moral dilemmas associated with notions of 'improvement' in Austen's work.

THE 'GENERAL'S IMPROVING HAND'

What disappoints Catherine the most about Northanger is the 'General's improving hand' (p. 173). The ancient kitchen of the convent, for example, is 'rich [and the word is surely important] in the massy walls and smoke of former days, and in the stoves and hot closets of the present'. It is full of every possible modern invention to aid the cooks in their 'spacious [another significant word] theatre' (p. 173). The display of wealth and commodities is everywhere. And the General is following in the footsteps of his father, who had one decaying side of the quadrangle replaced with something that 'was not only new, but declared itself to be so' (p. 174). Architectural debates over the renovation of old buildings in the eighteenth century led to renovation assuming political associations: the conservative desire to maintain and the progressive interest in dismantling or modernising. The General clearly places himself on the side of the latter. Keep this in mind when assessing Henry Tilney's vision of England in his lecture to Catherine at the end of the next chapter.

STUDY FOCUS: FEMALE SPACE

A03

Ellen Moers, who first coined the term 'female Gothic' with reference to Ann Radcliffe's work, writes in *Literary Women* (1976) that, inside castles, 'her heroines can scuttle miles along corridors, descend into dungeons, and explore secret chambers without chaperone, because the Gothic castle … is … an indoor and therefore freely female space' (p. 126). More recent critics, however, have emphasised the constraining nature of the **Gothic** castle in female Gothic. The female **protagonist** is transported out of her idyllic and secluded life and confined within a great house or castle under the authority of a powerful male figure. Within this labyrinthine space she is trapped and pursued.

The heroine's experiences within this Gothic space are represented as a journey leading towards her growth as an independent individual. As Catherine begins to script the story of Mrs Tilney in her mind, which reading of female Gothic would you find most appropriate here? Is the abbey as a Gothic space associated primarily with female growth and development or with female confinement?

CHECK THE BOOK **A03**

The Female Gothic: New Directions (2010), edited by Andrew Smith and Diana Wallace, contains a number of essays you may find useful, including discussions of the Northanger canon, bleeding nuns and Bluebeard's chamber, and considers such authors as Ann Radcliffe, Charlotte Brontë and Angela Carter.

GLOSSARY

173	**hot closets** cupboards with shelves in which prepared food could be kept hot, often with the use of steam
174	**pattened** pattens are protective overshoes, usually with a wooden sole
174	**dishabille** the state of being only partially or casually clothed

VOLUME TWO, CHAPTER 9

SUMMARY

- At church the next morning, Catherine sees a monument to the memory of Mrs Tilney erected by the General.
- The following day Eleanor agrees to show Catherine Mrs Tilney's room, but is prevented by the General calling Eleanor away.
- Catherine determines to see the room by herself.
- She enters the room and realises there is nothing abnormal to be found.
- Henry Tilney appears and questions her on her intentions in visiting the room.
- He realises Catherine's suspicions and the chapter ends with his lecture on her lack of judgement.

ANALYSIS

BLUEBEARD EMBODIED

Catherine scripts the story of Mrs Tilney in her mind with the aid of a variety of possible fictions, including Ann Radcliffe's *A Sicilian Romance* (1790), in which Mazzini imprisons his wife in an abandoned wing of his castle for fifteen years, after faking her funeral. In addition, the **trope** of the 'forbidden door' (p. 181) recurs in this chapter, with, this time, Bluebeard himself appearing in the 'dreaded figure' of General Tilney who, just as Eleanor's hand is upon the lock, calls out his daughter's name in loud resounding tones. Catherine experiences 'terror upon terror' (p. 180), but, like all **Gothic** heroines, she also continues to feel insatiable curiosity.

STUDY FOCUS: THE ROOM REVEALED A03

Catherine enters Mrs Tilney's room and is 'fixed … to the spot' (p. 182) by what she sees. This is no Gothic room of horrors, however, but a large and bright apartment, with – reflecting the General's delight in fashionable gadgets and inventions – all the comforts of a modern fireplace (a Bath stove) and elegant sash windows through which the 'warm beams' of the sun 'gaily poured' (p. 182). Against Gothic darkness she discovers light, instead of melancholia, gaiety, and instead of venerable age, modernity: the ancient rooms she expected turn out to be part of the modern wing. It is significant that in the humiliation that follows this discovery, Catherine sees two other doors in the chamber, but has 'no inclination to open either' (p. 182). She is curious no more.

BROKEN PROMISES

Claudia Johnson has argued in *Jane Austen: Women, Politics and the Novel* (1988) that breaking engagements and other promises is central to *Northanger Abbey*. Isabella is perhaps the most prominent promise breaker, with her promises repeatedly giving way to self-interest. Henry Tilney, with his usual concern for the niceties of language, may laugh at the **tautology** of a 'faithful promise' (p. 184) but, in this world, most promises are indeed hardly 'faithful'.

CHECK THE BOOK A03

In Radcliffe's *The Mysteries of Udolpho* (1794), Emily, lost in the corridors of Udolpho with her servant, comes across the secret room with the black veil: 'Oh! do not go in there ma'amselle,' said Annette, 'you will only lose yourself further.' 'Bring the light forward,' said Emily, 'we may possibly find our way through these rooms' (Vol. 2, Chapter 5).

CHECK THE BOOK A03

Compare the disappointment of Mrs Tilney's room with the Gothic spaces of the red room in Charlotte Brontë's *Jane Eyre* (another novel that draws on the story of Bluebeard) or the panelled bed in which Lockwood 'dreams' of a wailing ghost in Emily Brontë's *Wuthering Heights*.

EXTENDED COMMENTARY

VOLUME TWO, CHAPTER 9, P. 186

The passage begins with Henry completely astounded: Catherine has 'formed a surmise of such horror as I have hardly words to …'. For the first time, the master of language appears at a loss for words. His subsequent lecture is, nevertheless, a piece of wonderfully constructed **rhetoric** and, given the topic, this is important. He is shocked, and not his usual distanced and **ironic** self, but he nevertheless speaks in a beautifully balanced and authoritative manner appropriate to the voice of reason. Notice the repetition of words, particularly at the start of sentences, a strategy called **anaphora**, which produces emphasis on these first words, creating a sense of harmony as he proceeds. This is helped by a series of **rhetorical questions** which repeat similar sentence structures as in 'Does our education … / Do our laws' or 'where social and literary intercourse … / where every man is surrounded … / where roads and newspapers …'.

Henry directs how we should read throughout the novel, explaining texts and explaining people. Recall, for example, the moment when Eleanor misunderstands Catherine's claim that something very shocking will be coming out of London, and Henry's response: 'shall I make you understand each other' (p. 108). Nevertheless, perhaps we need to be wary of always accepting his position as the authoritative one, or conflating his views with those of Jane Austen. In particular, his position on England in this passage is worth investigating in some detail in the context of the Gothic.

'Remember the country and the age in which we live.' Henry, implicitly setting his England against a more primitive time and place, argues here that the English nation has been as much updated and improved as the abbey itself. It is a country in which the forces of reason and light – laws and education and Christian beliefs – have triumphed over the dark and archaic. In Henry's England, nothing remains secret: 'roads and newspapers lay every thing open'. In this world where everything is visible, Gothic atrocities such as the hiding away of an unloved wife cannot be committed.

It is worth noting that this is precisely the point underlying Gothic fiction of the eighteenth century: atrocities always take place in another country and a past time, and serve to set up the Protestant English world as a place of reason and civilisation against the irrational and the primitive of that other world. Henry rebukes Catherine, therefore, using the very standards and strategies of the novels that have deceived her. England, this country, is different from that 'other' country, and superior.

CHECK THE BOOK A03

Ian McEwan uses this passage from *Northanger Abbey* as the preface to his novel *Atonement* (2001), perhaps as a warning to the reader to beware as his main character Briony has an imagination as active as that of Catherine.

CONTEXT A04

In 1794, Habeas Corpus was suspended, making possible the imprisonment of political suspects without trial. Voluntary movements of citizens reported seditious activities and the government often used spies. Residents in Somerset even reported William Wordsworth and Samuel Taylor Coleridge to the government in 1796; they were suspected of being French spies.

CHECK THE BOOK **A03**

It is usually considered that Gothic was domesticated and brought into the contemporary world of middle-class England by such Victorian sensation writers as Wilkie Collins in *The Woman in White* (1860) and Mary Elizabeth Braddon in *Lady Audley's Secret* (1862). As *Northanger Abbey* demonstrates, however, Austen brought the Gothic home well before this.

This lecture has caused much debate among critics. Traditionally, it has been read as the culminating scene of Catherine's education: a young girl, seduced by her reading of literature into absurd imaginings, is rebuked by the male voice of reason that shows her the error of her ways. Henry argues that Catherine must give up her fantasies and move to a clearer understanding of what is probable. In *Some Words of Jane Austen* (1973), Stuart Tave, for example, argues that 'Henry's admonition to Catherine, which may seem terribly parochial, or even blindly self-satisfied, as though a happy exemption for serious moral problems were grated God's Englishmen, is, rather, an active direction that she rouse herself to the reality of moral problems' (pp. 62–3). In this reading, Catherine has been blind. She has imposed an explanation on her experiences at Northanger derived not from her observations of the complexities of life around her, but from a simple fiction.

For other critics, however, Henry's scornful dismissal of Catherine's **Gothic** fears is wrong. '"Common life"', as Tony Tanner argues in *Jane Austen* (1986), 'has proved to be capable of producing surprising uncommonness; anxiety may be a form of controlled alarm' (p. 73). This is based not just on what is to come, when the General comes to seem a true Montoni in ejecting Catherine from Northanger, but more generally on the way contemporary society reflects the sexual politics of the Gothic: that is, as the situations of both Eleanor and Mrs Tilney demonstrate, the powerlessness of women, a central issue in the Gothic novel, is a legal and economic truth in contemporary society and evident to all.

As a reader, then, Henry is deficient, because he cannot see the Gothic novel as anything more than a good read, something guaranteed to create the pleasurable experience of having one's 'hair standing on end the whole time' (p. 103). Indeed, some critics see him becoming the subject of **irony** here himself, in his too easy belief in the **ideology** about England as a world of light and reason.

Catherine, on the other hand, is a deficient reader because she takes things a little too literally: she imagines such Gothic atrocities as the murder and imprisonment of a wife, but is oblivious to the more real villainy going on around her. Nevertheless, it is also Catherine's reading that has taught her to fear the kind of **patriarchal** authority that the General represents in updated form. Catherine is not, as some have said, simply conflating the General with a Radcliffean villain; she is identifying something in his 'air and attitude' (p. 176) reminiscent of Montoni, and she is right. The General was a tyrant to his wife, he is a tyrant to his daughter, and he is, like Montoni with Emily, after Catherine's money.

As Claudia Johnson observes in *Jane Austen: Women, Politics and the Novel* (1988), *Northanger Abbey* is 'an alarming novel to the extent that it, in its own unassuming and matter-of-fact way, domesticates the gothic and brings its apparent excesses into the drawing rooms of "the midland countries of England"' while the convention of the happy ending towards which the novel now begins to move 'draws our attention away from the "all too legitimate" causes for alarm' (p. 42).

VOLUME TWO, CHAPTER 10

SUMMARY

- Catherine understands that she has been deluded by her reading.
- She considers Henry right in asserting such things do not happen in England.
- A letter arrives from James saying the engagement with Isabella has been broken and that Captain Tilney was involved.
- Catherine assumes Isabella is to marry Captain Tilney.
- She tells Henry and Eleanor.

ANALYSIS

VISIONS OF ROMANCE ARE OVER

For the fourth time Catherine's **Gothic** imaginings have been deflated: we've seen this in the abbey itself, the chest, the cabinet and lastly with Mrs Tilney. In each case Catherine anticipated and sought out evidence of dreadful deeds, only to be humiliated by the apparent absurdity of her expectations and fears. Now, however, Henry's lecture is decisive: 'The visions of romance were over' (p. 187). And it is not just her Gothic fancies that are at issue here. Catherine has grown increasingly aware that marriage to Henry is a possibility but, after being admonished by him in such a way, she wonders if that particular romance is threatened too.

STUDY FOCUS: THE MIDLAND COUNTIES OF ENGLAND **A04**

Is Catherine's dismissal of Radcliffe a sign of her newly developed maturity? Or is this just Catherine repeating Henry's opinions? Recall their first meeting when he says, 'Shall I tell you what you ought to say?' (p. 26). Has Catherine's education culminated in precisely this – saying what Henry thinks?

Catherine's thoughts, as she repeats Henry's points to herself, become somewhat comical as Austen has Catherine avoid extremities of all kinds – ideological, emotional or geographical. 'Catherine dared not doubt beyond her own country, and even of that, if hard pressed, would have yielded the northern and western extremities' (p. 188). While 'in the central part of England' (p. 188) she believes there is security, she would hesitate to speak for Scotland, Ireland and Wales. As Stuart Tave has argued in *Some Words of Jane Austen* (1973), Catherine, who is from the 'midland' counties of England – something with both geographical and ideological implications – now takes up the middle position.

We might also want to consider if it is precisely true that her imaginings have been all 'a voluntary, self-created delusion' (p. 188). And, finally, how do we reconcile Catherine's conclusions with her later judgement on the General (p. 230)?

VOLUME TWO, CHAPTER 11

SUMMARY

- Plans are made to dine with Henry at Woodston.
- Henry leaves to make preparations.
- Catherine prefers the village of Woodston and Henry's parsonage to the far grander abbey.
- The General makes it clear that he expects Catherine to be the mistress of Woodston.
- Catherine wishes she were equally sure of Henry's intentions.

CONTEXT **A04**

Jane Austen spent the first twenty-five years of her life in her father's parsonage in Steventon in Hampshire. Many of her other heroines end up married and living in parsonages, including Fanny in *Mansfield Park* (1814) and Elinor in *Sense and Sensibility* (1811).

ANALYSIS

THE GENERAL'S ORDERS

More evidence of the General's controlling nature is provided as plans are made for the excursion to Woodston. The General initially professes there is no need to fix a day and that Henry must not put himself to any trouble in providing a meal. By the end of his remarks (p. 197) he has, however, not just set the day as Wednesday, but also fixed the time of arrival for precisely a quarter to one. Henry, knowing his father's expectations, almost immediately leaves to begin preparations for an elaborate dinner. Catherine is perplexed: 'why he should say one thing so positively, and mean another all the while, was most unaccountable! How were people, at that rate, to be understood' (p. 198). In the General's tendency towards double-speak, he bears no small resemblance to the Thorpes.

While at Woodston, the General makes clear his intention that Henry and Catherine should marry. He has, for example, considered knocking down the cottage among the trees – another sign of his improving hand – but, with Catherine's expression of delight, 'The cottage remains' (p. 200). Even Catherine cannot miss the point, and it produces some embarrassing moments for her.

STUDY FOCUS: WOODSTON AS DOMESTIC IDYLL **A02**

The abbey Catherine so longed to visit is 'no more to her now than any other house' (p. 198), and when General Tilney, Eleanor and Catherine go to dine with Henry at Woodston, it would seem that the **Gothic** has completely given way to domestic idyll. Rather than longing for chilly, dark winding staircases, dust and cobwebs, Catherine finds herself admiring the prettiness and neatness of the village of Woodston, and the prettiness and the comforts of the parsonage. Notice how many times the word 'prettiness' is repeated (pp. 199, 200, 201). Woodston is set in clear opposition to the ostentatious grandeur of Northanger, and Catherine seems to be looking at Woodston as her potential home. But it is soon after we are lulled into anticipating a concluding domestic idyll that the Gothic will return, in an updated form, and with a vengeance.

GLOSSARY

199 **chandler's shops** a chandler was originally a dealer in candles, but the term had come to be applied to any shop that specialised in a particular kind of merchandise

VOLUME TWO, CHAPTER 12

SUMMARY

- Catherine receives a letter from Isabella who has clearly been discarded by Captain Tilney.
- She attempts to persuade Catherine to intervene with James.
- Catherine is indignant and ashamed of ever being Isabella's friend.

ANALYSIS

LOSING AT COMMERCE

The significance of Isabella previously playing a 'pool of commerce' now becomes quite clear. As in the card game, where players can try to improve their hands by swapping one or more of their own cards for a table card, so Isabella, once she realises that James is not very wealthy, has tried to swap him for a better card, Captain Tilney, and she has lost. She now attempts to feign ignorance of the problem: James seemed 'so uncomfortable when he went away, with a cold, or something that affected his spirits' (p. 203). This is obviously a desperate attempt to recoup her losses, and Catherine is wrong to dismiss Isabella as a 'vain coquette' (p. 204). She is playing a more serious game than that.

Isabella, the female character who is the most active player in the marriage market, is punished and left with nothing while – notice again the double standard – Captain Tilney is considered blameless. Isabella is doomed to fail in a society where women's power extends – at the very most – no further than, in Henry's terms, 'the power of refusal' (p. 74). There is a hint in her letter that suggests she had made one final play the previous evening and failed when she refers to going to the theatre with the Hodges – 'for a frolic, at half-price' (p. 203). Consider whether that financial detail might be significant. We might recall that when James went to Fullerton to get his father's consent, Isabella claimed she would not dance, even though 'Charles Hodges will plague me to death I dare say' (p. 124). If Hodges was, as we might suspect, a final gamble that failed, this letter is the product of that final failure, a last attempt to recoup her losses.

STUDY FOCUS: ISABELLA'S LANGUAGE **A02**

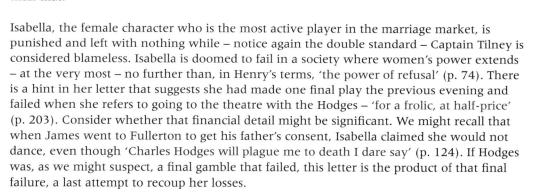

The letter provides an excellent compact opportunity for close analysis of Isabella's use of language. All her most typical traits can be found here, so markedly that even Catherine recognises 'its inconsistencies, contradictions, and falsehood' (p. 203). Try to identify examples of the language of excess or **hyperbole** – 'a thousand apologies', 'vile place' (p. 202) – and of double-speak – the use of language to deceive through concealment or misrepresentation. Notice also Isabella's typical chaotic speech, which veers from 'the only man I ever did or could love' to the frightful spring hats (p. 202) in a complete confusion of categories. She is unable to stay focused enough for her strategies to work.

CHECK THE BOOK **A04**

For an interesting analysis of the use of card games in Austen's fiction, see Alistair Duckworth's 'Spillikins, Paper Ships, Riddles, Conundrums, and Cards', in John Halperin, ed., *Jane Austen: Bicentenary Essays* (1975).

VOLUME TWO, CHAPTER 13

SUMMARY

- The General goes to London.
- While Henry is away at Woodston, General Tilney returns; he speaks privately with Eleanor.
- The General orders Catherine to leave Northanger the next morning.
- Catherine is humiliated at what is clearly an intentional insult and cannot understand how she has offended.
- Eleanor, horrified but helpless, provides her with money for her journey home.

ANALYSIS

ANOTHER KIND OF CARRIAGE

The depth of the insult to Catherine is encapsulated in the means of transport. Sending her in a hack chaise – the equivalent of hiring a taxi today – rather than sending her in his own carriage is an insult and, as we later realise, a statement on what he considers her lowered status. It is when Catherine sees the public transport in which she must ride, unchaperoned and without servant to attend her, that she feels the depth of the insult: 'Catherine's colour rose at the sight of it' (p. 213).

WOMEN'S 'POWER'

Attempting to explain her inability to prevent Catherine's expulsion from Northanger, Eleanor observes she is only 'nominal mistress' of the house: 'my real power is nothing' (p. 210). Women's vulnerability in a world where they have no legal protection is consequently emphasised not only through Catherine but also through her friend. For Henry, violence within the home in his enlightened England may be inconceivable, but the home is no place of security for Catherine, and only a prison of sorts for Eleanor.

CRITICAL VIEWPOINT A03

'Rather than rejecting the gothic conventions she burlesques, Austen is very clearly criticizing female gothic in order to reinvest it with authority. … Austen's heroine is defined as a reader, and in her narrative she blunders on more significant, if less melodramatic, truths as potentially destructive as any in Mrs Radcliffe's fictions' (Gilbert and Gubar, *The Madwoman in the Attic*, 1979, p. 284).

STUDY FOCUS: CAUSES FOR ALARM   A02

The arrival of Eleanor to convey the General's decision to Catherine is marked by a return to **Gothic** suggestiveness. Catherine hears the noise of something moving near her door, tentatively touching it, and a slight movement of the lock that suggests a hand upon it. Notice how all the words associated with Catherine's previous Gothic visions momentarily return: 'fancy', 'alarm', 'trembled', 'imagination' (p. 208). While Catherine controls her imagination, the language nevertheless signals some connections to her previous assumptions about General Tilney – and this is most appropriate, given the message Eleanor must convey.

Consider also the passage describing Catherine lying awake all night, listening to the high winds and the noises it produces in the old house, 'without curiosity or terror' (p. 212). Notice the way in which the language connects this night to the night of her arrival, and yet, instead of superstitious fears keeping her awake, it is the 'contemplation of actual and natural evil' (p. 212). All this is to prepare us for Catherine's ultimate judgement on the General when she discovers the reason for her ejection from Northanger (p. 230).

VOLUME TWO, CHAPTER 14

SUMMARY

- Catherine returns home to Fullerton in a hack post-chaise.
- The Morlands are unhappy with the way their daughter has been treated but relieved that she has arrived home safely.
- Mrs Morland and Catherine call upon Mrs Allen.

ANALYSIS

THE TRAVELLING HEROINE

In the previous chapter, Eleanor had made clear her concerns for Catherine's safety as well as her concerns about the impropriety of such treatment, and the dangers of this journey are also emphasised here. Catherine may be oblivious to them, but it is clearly not safe for a woman, even in the 'central part of England' (p. 188), to travel seventy miles alone. Mrs Morland, more sensible than imaginative, has no 'romantic alarms' (p. 218) about her daughter's experiences, and philosophically concludes 'it is no matter now; Catherine is safe at home' (p. 219). Nevertheless, their reactions show the serious nature of the General 'forcing her on such a measure' (p. 218).

STUDY FOCUS: NARRATIVE VOICE **A01**

If the characters focus primarily on Catherine's safety, the **narrator**, like Catherine herself, focuses more on Catherine's humiliation. The narrator becomes as **intrusive** in this chapter as she was at the start, and increasingly emphasises the fact that this is a novel she is writing, describing herself as 'the author' and 'the contriver' of the story and 'biographer' of 'my heroine' (p. 217).

Catherine may be a more plausible kind of heroine than found in the sentimental **romances** Austen **parodies**, but she is still a work of fiction. The narrator's controlling hand is emphasised as she makes clear that, since her heroine returns in disgrace and not triumph, she will allow no lingering on the journey through Fullerton: she will ensure the post-boy drives Catherine swiftly through the village, out of the sight of prying eyes and into the safety of her parents' home.

> **CRITICAL VIEWPOINT A03**
>
> Radcliffean Gothic appears when the idea emerges that 'romance, by its very inclusion of the marvellous or the apparently marvellous, can reveal the unpleasant truth about real life in a way impossible in the referential narratives of **realist novelists**' (E. J. Clery, *The Rise of Supernatural Fiction*, 1995, p. 129).

VOLUME TWO, CHAPTER 15

SUMMARY

- Catherine is unhappy and listless.
- Mrs Morland goes to look for a book and when she returns finds Henry with Catherine.
- Catherine accompanies Henry on a walk to the Allens and he proposes marriage.
- Henry explains that the General had thought Catherine wealthier than she was. John Thorpe had initially misled the General, but, angry at Catherine's lack of interest in him, had subsequently exaggerated the Morlands' lack of wealth and connection.

ANALYSIS

A LACK OF IMAGINATION

If Catherine has been led into an excess of imagination, Mrs Morland seems to possess none at all. Sensible she may be, but she is completely unable to understand her daughter's feelings, and assumes she has been spoilt by the luxuries of Northanger. We could possibly connect this with Henry's comment upon Catherine's inability to understand or imagine how others might think and act.

STUDY FOCUS: A NEW CIRCUMSTANCE IN ROMANCE A03

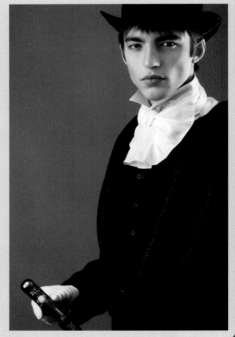

Once more deflating the conventions of sentimental **romance**, the **narrator** admits that 'a persuasion of [Catherine's] partiality for him had been the only cause of [Henry] giving her a serious thought' (p. 227). Michael Kramp, in *Disciplining Love: Austen and the Modern Man* (2007), argues that Henry's 'strong adherence to the doctrine of rationality protects him from the potentially overwhelming powers of love. … he will not allow the irrational or sublime to affect his behaviour, and even his climactic decision to disobey the authority of his father and travel to the Morlands' home is based upon reason' (p. 11). Do you agree with this? In what sense is his decision to disobey based upon reason?

It is quite revealing to compare this scene with the equivalent, far more passionate, scene of proposal in either of the films of *Northanger Abbey*, updated to appeal to a modern audience. Austen's lovers are often quite restrained on the surface, but perhaps there is no relationship quite as stripped of romance as this one. Compare this scene with some of the other final love scenes in Austen's works, such as when Elizabeth Bennet accepts Mr Darcy in *Pride and Prejudice*.

CHECK THE BOOK A03

It is revealing to compare the way in which Austen deals with love with the way in which Emily Brontë deals with love in *Wuthering Heights*. Compare her Catherine and Heathcliff with this Catherine and Henry.

THE GENERAL EXPLAINED

Once the General's economic motives in both his pursuit of Catherine and his ejection of Catherine from Northanger are made clear, Catherine feels that 'in suspecting General Tilney of either murdering or shutting up his wife, she had scarcely sinned against his character, or magnified his cruelty' (p. 230). In pursuing Catherine for her supposed inheritance, the General does behave something like a Montoni, who pursues Emily for hers, and in his treatment of his wife, his children and Catherine, he reveals himself to be a tyrant as controlling as any **Gothic** villain. There has indeed been a mystery at Northanger Abbey, and she has been the 'heroine' at the centre of it. Gothic, then, is not just a foil to the domestic and ordinary world of the characters; persecution and entrapment are as much a part of this society as they are of any Gothic fiction.

GLOSSARY

229   **rhodomontade** vain and empty boasting

REVISION FOCUS: TASK 4   **A01**

How far do you agree with the statement below?

● *Northanger Abbey* ultimately favours the imagination over reason.

Try writing an opening paragraph for an essay based on this discussion point. Set out your argument clearly.

CRITICAL VIEWPOINT **A01**

In *Narcissistic Narrative: The Metafictional Paradox* (1980), Linda Hutcheon suggests that '**Parodic** art both is a deviation from the norm and includes that norm within itself as background material' (p. 50).

VOLUME TWO, CHAPTER 16

SUMMARY

- The Morlands give their consent to the marriage, but only on the condition that the General also gives his consent.
- Eleanor marries a wealthy man.
- In his consequent good humour the General agrees to the marriage of Catherine and Henry.

ANALYSIS

CONSULT YOUR SENSE OF THE PROBABLE

The **realist novel** offers the notion of transparency, the illusion that we are being given direct access to a real world that encourages us to forget we are reading a fiction. This is completely deflated by Austen as once more the **narrator** reminds us that we are reading a work of fiction. The very materiality of the book becomes an issue as the reader sees 'in the tell-tale compression of the pages before them, that we are all hastening together to perfect felicity' (p. 233). While the narrator's reference to 'perfect felicity' suggests she is bound, by convention, to conclude happily with marriage, she simultaneously makes clear that, as the author of this fiction, she has the power to do whatever she likes. Detail is unnecessary given our knowledge of the conventions, and all is reduced to 'the bells rang and everyone smiled' (p. 235). If Henry urged Catherine to consult her own sense of the probable, it is something the reader should do too. Austen's wildly improbable conclusion, full of arch and knowing commentary from the narrator who busily tidies up all the loose ends, sinks us in the improbable.

> **CONTEXT** A04
>
> Deus ex machina, Latin for 'god from the machine', is a phrase first popularised by the Roman poet Horace who instructed writers not to resort to contrived endings. A representative use of deus ex machina is in Euripedes's tragedy *Medea* in which a dragon-drawn chariot arrives from the gods to save Medea, who has just murdered her own children, from the wrath of her husband Jason.

STUDY FOCUS: ENTER PRINCE CHARMING A02

First, there is the eleventh-hour introduction of 'the most charming young man in the world' (p. 234) to save Eleanor from her most probable fate of ending up an old maid in her tyrannical father's home. No more need be said, says the narrator. Then, in one of those typically self-conscious gestures, she adds in parenthesis, 'aware that the rules of composition forbid the introduction of a [new] character' (p. 234), that this is the very man who left behind the collection of washing bills. It is a kind of **deus ex machina**, and also a cliché, and the narrator refuses to elaborate on that young man's virtues, leaving the cliché as nothing more than cliché. Claiming to conform to the rules of novel-writing, the narrator consequently introduces more improbability. What other examples can you find in this final chapter that show the narrator's self-consciousness about this being a book that we are reading?

HAPPILY EVER AFTER

In considering the fate of Eleanor, it is useful to remember Isabella's conflation of wealth, power and choice. 'Had I the command of millions, were I mistress of the whole world, your brother would be my only choice' (p. 114). Isabella, with no money, believes it would enable her to choose rather than just be chosen, but Eleanor's situation shows this is not actually true. Although the narrator asserts (and notice the repetition) that she is given the 'home of her choice and the man of her choice' (p. 233), it is chance and not choice that results in the marriage.

It is certainly true for men in this particular world: wealth equals power equals choice. For women, however, wealth can, in fact, be a problem. The knowledge of a long-standing attachment between Eleanor and a gentleman of 'inferior' situation emerges only in the final chapter and it is only because of his fairy-tale 'unexpected accession to title and fortune' (p. 234) that he is able to ask Eleanor to marry him. Her wealth and position impede rather than aid the relationship. She has no power to choose him: for her, money does not equate to power.

CRITICAL VIEWPOINT A02

In *The Art of Fiction* (1993), David Lodge writes: 'Novels are narratives, and narrative, whatever its medium – words, film, strip-cartoon – holds the interest of an audience by raising questions in their minds, and delaying the answers' (p. 30).

STUDY FOCUS: PARENTAL TYRANNY OR FILIAL DISOBEDIENCE? A01

The novel ends with what appears to be some kind of moral: 'I leave it to be settled by whomsoever it may concern, whether the tendency of this work be altogether to recommend parental tyranny, or reward filial disobedience' (p. 235). This is an ending that has left many readers dissatisfied. What do you think Austen means by this? Is it that the General's opposition brought about the happy ending, or that Henry's defiance of his father brings about the happy ending?

CHARACTERS

CATHERINE MORLAND

WHO IS CATHERINE MORLAND?

- Catherine is the daughter of a clergyman in Fullerton and is invited by her neighbours Mr and Mrs Allen to accompany them to Bath.
- She becomes friends with Isabella Thorpe and she meets Henry Tilney, with whom she falls in love, and his sister Eleanor.
- Catherine is enthusiastically pursued by Isabella's brother, John Thorpe, in whom she is uninterested.
- General Tilney invites her to Northanger Abbey, under the false impression that she is an heiress. Here she plays out a series of mock **Gothic** adventures before being evicted by the General, who has discovered the truth.
- Henry comes to Fullerton to propose, she accepts, obstacles are overcome and they are married.

THE ARTLESS HEROINE

Catherine, as heroine, falls far short of the improbable 'standards' of the sentimental novel. She has none of the typical affectations, and – until caught up in Gothic plots – tends to be a sensible and balanced individual. She is an ingénue, endearingly innocent and wholesome, which sets her in opposition to the always artful Isabella. It is these qualities that attract Henry Tilney. But Catherine is also naive. Forthright and direct herself, she is bewildered by the subtleties and duplicity of characters like Isabella and General Tilney. She assumes everyone's motives and interests are just like her own, demonstrating a lack of imagination and a touch of self-centredness.

STUDY FOCUS: LESSONS FROM ISABELLA · A02

Isabella provides Catherine's education in Volume One, initiating her into the world of fashion, shopping and Gothic novels, and Catherine's speech shows this influence as she gradually takes on some of the extravagances associated with her friend. Ultimately, however, the most important lesson she learns through her association with Isabella is the deceptiveness of surfaces: she learns to see through Isabella's shallow artifice. When do you think she begins to exert her independence from Isabella and to think for herself? What are the key moments in the movement away from Isabella's influence?

> **CRITICAL VIEWPOINT** · A02
>
> David Lodge writes in *The Art of Fiction* (1993), 'It has been said that all novels are essentially about the passage from innocence to experience, about discovering the reality that underlies appearances. It is not surprising, therefore, that stylistic and dramatic **irony** are all-pervasive in this form of literature' (p. 179).

LESSONS FROM HENRY

Natural goodness is not enough, Austen shows. Artlessness can be dangerous, truth is more complicated than it seems, and Catherine must learn to discriminate and develop her judgement. Whether this is something she is taught by Henry, or whether she learns for herself through experience, has been a matter of critical debate. Perhaps there is some truth to both positions.

Catherine must renounce her Gothic imaginings and extravagances and assume the balanced, reasonable perspective – and language – of Henry. But learning is not simply a matter of internalising the perspectives of others. When Catherine, for example, listens to Henry lecture on the **picturesque**, she is so eager to please that she dismisses the whole of Bath 'as unworthy to make part of a landscape' (p. 107), and becomes the target of some gentle **satire** from the **narrator** (see also **Themes**, on **Education**).

DEVELOPING JUDGEMENT

Catherine's real moment of education, perhaps, is when she comes to the conclusion that, Montoni or not (and Henry's rebuke aside), the General is just not a very nice man at all. Catherine learns to be more discriminating and to rely on her own judgement. It is only after learning these lessons that she gets her reward in marriage to Henry, and all the benefits in terms of money and status that this involves.

KEY QUOTATIONS: CATHERINE   A01

- Catherine on seeing Eleanor: 'guided only by what was simple and probable, it had never entered her head that Mr. Tilney could be married' (p. 52).

- Catherine's unintentional satire: 'I cannot speak well enough to be unintelligible' (p. 126).

- Catherine's Gothic imaginings begin: 'she could not entirely subdue the hope of some traditional legends, some awful memorials of an injured and ill-fated nun' (p. 134).

CONTEXT   A04

In Jane Austen's time, a woman had very few legal rights. Indeed, after marriage she had no legal status at all. According to the Law of Coverture: 'the very being or legal existence of a woman is suspended during marriage – or at least incorporated and consolidated into that of her husband under whose wing and protection and cover she performs everything'. Everything she had was under her husband's legal control. If widowed, she had no right to her children unless he had named her guardian; if the couple were separated, the husband had legal possession of the children.

HENRY TILNEY

WHO IS HENRY TILNEY?

- Henry is a clergyman, the second son of General Tilney and brother to Eleanor and Frederick.
- He meets and courts Catherine in Bath and becomes her mentor before eventually marrying her.

AN UNCONVENTIONAL HERO

Henry is as unconventional a hero as Catherine is an unconventional heroine. He is not quite handsome, is dominated by his father, rather odd in the **ironic** playfulness of his conversation, and perhaps somewhat feminised: consider his knowledge about Gothic novels and muslins. His knowledge of the **Gothic** is more knowing than Catherine's, based on an understanding of its conventions rather than on naive enthusiasm.

CLERGYMAN AND MANLINESS

Henry may also seem an unusual hero in that he is a clergyman, but Austen's heroes – consider Edward in *Sense and Sensibility*, Edmund in *Mansfield Park* – often are. And this goes against the idea that Henry is feminised since Austen, as Robert Miles notes in *Jane Austen* (2003), associates the clergy with manly behaviour because 'manly behaviour for her was … connected to social responsibility rather than such qualities as physical prowess' (p. 113).

STUDY FOCUS: THE VOICE OF REASON? A04

Critical opinion is strongly divided on the question of Henry. Some find him the voice of good sense and reason, teaching Catherine through play, and encouraging her development through posing questions and puzzles she must work out for herself. Others consider he is a more refined version of the bully embodied in John Thorpe, putting words into Catherine's mouth and frequently silencing her. Which position do you find most convincing?

GRADE BOOSTER A01

In *Northanger Abbey*, many characters say one thing while they mean quite another. You should be able to carefully distinguish, however, Isabella's duplicity from Henry's irony, even though both depend on a kind of double-speak.

HENRY AS IRONIC COMMENTATOR

Henry affects the distanced and yet tolerant and often jocular tone of the **narrator**, and he has sometimes been considered to speak for the author (see also **Part Four: Language**, on **Irony**). The similarity between them is strengthened by some of the opinions that Henry expresses: like the narrator, for example, he offers a defence of the novel. But none of her characters can ever be said to speak directly for Austen. In his 'niceness' about language he may be too pedantic and, in his rebuke to Catherine, too dogmatic. His idea of an England ruled by light and reason is as much a fiction as Catherine's assumptions about dark Gothic deeds at Northanger. Henry too has things to learn.

KEY QUOTATIONS: HENRY A01

- Catherine on Henry: '"How can you," said Catherine, laughing, "be so –" she had almost said, strange' (p. 28).
- Henry on the analogy between dancing and matrimony: 'in both, man has the advantage of choice, woman only the power of refusal' (p. 74).
- Rebuking Catherine: 'Remember the country and the age in which we live' (p. 186).

ELEANOR TILNEY

WHO IS ELEANOR TILNEY?

- Eleanor is the sister of Henry and the daughter of General Tilney.
- Her unexpected marriage in the final chapter paves the way for the marriage of Henry and Catherine.

ELEANOR AND FRIENDSHIP

Eleanor functions in part as a contrast to Isabella. Like Isabella, Eleanor is older and wiser than Catherine; unlike Isabella, she does not take advantage and try to manipulate her. If Isabella is the false friend of Volume One, always putting self-interest first, Eleanor is the true friend of Volume Two, defending Catherine when Henry teases her. Although Eleanor is powerless to stop her father evicting Catherine from Northanger, she helps as much as she can by lending her money.

GOOD BREEDING

Eleanor, full of 'good sense and good breeding' (p. 54), is also set in opposition to Isabella through descriptions of her manners. If Isabella is constantly going against social convention, chasing young men, going on unchaperoned carriage rides, Eleanor is the epitome of propriety. In the move from Isabella to Eleanor, we see fictional poses being replaced by social manners. The word most frequently applied to Eleanor is 'elegant', forming a contrast with the vulgarity of Isabella and suggesting the difference in their rank and wealth.

STUDY FOCUS: WOMEN AND POWER · A03

Eleanor, however, is completely powerless, indeed, ultimately as powerless as Isabella to effect any changes in her situation, and much more passive in accepting her fate than Isabella. Eleanor may possess all the virtues valued in Austen's world, but her rank and wealth put her too far above the man she loves. Inheritances for women like Eleanor are there to promote their marriages and to ally their families with others of at least equal rank and wealth. Consequently, she can only ultimately marry when the man she loves miraculously inherits a fortune and a title. Catherine may play the Gothic heroine, but Eleanor, in a sense, turns out to be one. Her mother is dead, and, under the domination of her father, Eleanor is isolated and basically confined to the abbey until released 'from all the evils of such a home as Northanger' (p. 233) through marriage. Notice the Gothic inflections here in the use of that term 'evil'. However, Eleanor is a very passive version of the Gothic heroine. Catherine, in contrast, shows the curiosity and spark that are associated with such Radcliffean heroines as Emily.

CRITICAL VIEWPOINT · A03

In considering the fate of Eleanor, Diane Hoeveler argues in *Gothic Feminism* (1998) that one of the aims of Austen's Gothic **parody** is to 'inflate the importance of issues explored in women's literature under the cover of deflating the excesses of such literature' (p. 125).

KEY QUOTATIONS: ELEANOR · A01

- The narrator on Eleanor: 'her air, though it had not all the decided pretension, the resolute stillishness of Miss Thorpe's, had more real elegance' (p. 54).
- Eleanor to Catherine: 'you must have been long enough in this house to see that I am but a nominal mistress of it, that my real power is nothing' (p. 210).

GENERAL TILNEY

WHO IS GENERAL TILNEY?

- General Tilney, father of Henry, Frederick and Eleanor, is the owner of Northanger Abbey.
- Tilney is a wealthy landowner. He is highly materialistic and first courts then rejects Catherine as a suitable wife for his son Henry. He accepts her when Eleanor's fortunes improve.

A VILLAIN

For much of the novel, General Tilney actually does quite the opposite of what one expects of the villain in either **Gothic** or sentimental **romance**. Rather than serving as an impediment to the courtship of the hero and heroine, he actively encourages it. However, in being a tyrannical father and a rather uncaring husband, he comes to seem more and more like the villains that Catherine has read about. His active pursuit of her for what he assumes is her impressive inheritance only links him more closely to such characters as Montoni in *The Mysteries of Udolpho*, whose interest in Emily is prompted only by the size of her inheritance.

STUDY FOCUS: THE MODERN VILLAIN **A04**

What also make the General a villain, however, are issues more specific to Jane Austen's world. His complete lack of morals and manners is demonstrated when he evicts Catherine, sending her seventy miles home – an eleven-hour trip – with no attention paid to her safety or comfort: no servant, no money. Insisting she leaves the next morning, which involves travelling on a Sunday, is particularly offensive since Catherine is a clergyman's daughter. He is the perfect product of the materialistic consumer culture, with his rampant individualism and a modernising zeal that sweeps aside everything in its way. It has also been suggested that the General, who spends his night poring over political pamphlets, is part of the state apparatus for monitoring political dissent: a state tyrant, then, as well as a domestic one (see also **Themes**, on **Consumer culture**).

THE GENERAL AND ISABELLA

In terms of social standing, the General and Isabella occupy quite different positions. But Austen always queries simple **dichotomies**. Just as the proliferation of consumer goods in Isabella's hunting grounds, Bath, is duplicated in the General's abbey, the two also share character traits. Like Isabella, the General is characterised by duplicity. His politeness is a form of bullying, his modesty is assumed. He is also materialistic like Isabella, and his professions of disinterest on the subject of money every bit as outrageous as hers. As his pride in his porcelain tea set, his modern kitchen, his hothouses and pinery suggests, he defines and assesses himself, and others, on the basis of possessions. While Isabella dreams of making an elaborate show, he has the wealth to put this into practice. His insistence on conspicuous displays of consumption is even demonstrated by the dinner at Woodston that takes Henry three days to prepare.

KEY QUOTATIONS: THE GENERAL **A01**

- On Northanger Abbey: 'The General's improving hand had not loitered here' (p. 173).
- Catherine on the General: 'It was the air and attitude of a Montoni!' (p. 176).

ISABELLA THORPE

WHO IS ISABELLA THORPE?

- Isabella is the eldest daughter of the widowed Mrs Thorpe.
- Thinking the Morlands are wealthier than they are, Isabella makes friends with Catherine in Bath and becomes engaged to James.
- When Captain Tilney appears to be a financially better prospect, Isabella tries and fails to catch him.

THE MOBILE ANTI-HEROINE

Isabella is the most entertaining of all the characters, and one of the more complex. Her aim is to make an advantageous marriage, both for herself and, if possible, for her brother: she wants to move up in the world, and to 'fix' a good husband. It is then appropriate that Isabella is the most mobile and unfixed character in the novel, completely at home in the consumer-driven world of Bath, constantly criss-crossing the town, pursuing young men under the guise of looking at hats, and always on the look-out for the best places to see and be seen. This mobility can be seen in her language: linguistic confusion seems to be her forte (see also **Part Four: Language**).

SENTIMENTAL HEROINE

Isabella is a poseur; she performs the role of the heroine of sentimental romance, whose primary characteristic is the intensity of her feelings. But her extravagant language and professions of strong feeling function only to mask her materialistic nature and her social ambitions (see also **Part Four: Language**). Isabella repeatedly attempts to cast Catherine into a role in the script she is performing, but Catherine simply does not understand Isabella's innuendo and tends to respond 'only by a look of wondering ignorance' (p. 112). For an example, read the paragraph in which Isabella claims she has seen a young man looking at Catherine and is sure he is in love with her (p. 40).

> **CHECK THE BOOK** **A03**
>
> Isabella anticipates the more famous Victorian fictional social climber: the delightfully devious Becky Sharp of W. M. Thackeray's *Vanity Fair* (1847–8).

STUDY FOCUS: ISABELLA'S MORALITY **A02**

Isabella ends up unmarried and alone; she cannot be taken into the society she aspires to join because she has not learned the lessons of respect and compassion; she has, in Austen's sense, no manners, no propriety. She is also considered vulgar because she takes an active role in the marriage market. Catherine, of course, is also in the marriage market, but she is unconscious of her role within it. Isabella understands herself to be a commodity, and at the same time attempts to be a 'shopper', choosing for herself. If we consider the position of a poor and unmarried woman at the time, we might come closer to sympathising with Isabella, but does the novel encourage this, or does it simply punish Isabella for her vulgarity and lack of morality? We might also ask why, although Austen shows so little sympathy for Isabella's position, readers today often confess a soft spot for the character and find her far more engaging than Catherine or Eleanor.

> **GRADE BOOSTER** **A02**
>
> Consider how other characters are set against each other in this novel, and how this contributes to the structuring of the plot. Isabella is set in opposition to both Catherine and Eleanor, for example, and there are three sister–brother pairs that can be compared and contrasted.

KEY QUOTATIONS: ISABELLA **A01**

- Isabella's pose as sentimental heroine: 'I believe my feelings are stronger than any body's; I am sure they are too strong for my own peace' (p. 94).
- Isabella's typical exaggeration: 'I have an hundred things to say to you' (p. 38).
- Isabella's ambitions: 'a carriage at her command, a new name on her tickets, and a brilliant exhibition of hoop rings on her finger' (p. 116).

JOHN THORPE

WHO IS JOHN THORPE?

- John is the brother of Isabella and one of the three sons of Mrs Thorpe.
- He is studying at Oxford, where he becomes friends with Catherine's brother James.
- John attempts to court Catherine with an eye on what he believes to be her considerable wealth.
- He first boasts about Catherine's supposed wealth to General Tilney and then, when she rejects him and he discovers the truth, reveals to the General that Catherine is not the Allens' heir.

ANOTHER VILLAIN

John is a **parody** of the libertine villain of sentimental **romance**. Although he 'abducts' Catherine in his carriage, it is only to go on a tourist excursion. Stout, plain and clumsy, he nevertheless attempts to present himself as a man of the world. In his speech he affects the role of the dandy or man of fashion: it is peppered with profanities and slang, but his bluster only emphasises his vulgarity. He is a braggart and a bore, constantly talking about the prices of things, about bargains that he thinks he has made, and so revealing his greed and ambition. Both James and the **narrator** describe him as a 'rattle', as someone who rattles on about nothing. He 'talks', as the narrator notes, rather than has a conversation (p. 64). He has no manners, is rude to his mother and sisters, and is as self-absorbed as his sister Isabella. And, like Isabella, he is a liar and has a tendency to **hyperbole**. Consequently he does much damage to Catherine, first through his boasting and then through the lies he tells to General Tilney.

A HORSE WITHOUT VICE

John offers his own version of Isabella's penchant for fashionable jargon, and, also like Isabella, inappropriately applies a moral register. Of his placid horse he boasts, for example, that he is 'full of spirits, playful as can be, but there is no vice in him' (p. 61), and on novels he remarks that there has 'not been a tolerably decent one come out since Tom Jones, except the Monk' (p. 47), both considered risqué and far from 'decent'.

STUDY FOCUS: CHARACTER AND METONYMY   A02

John Thorpe provides an excellent example of how Austen creates character through **metonymic** associations, that is, he may be a relatively flat character in many ways, but he still comes to life for the reader through the things that are repeatedly associated with him, such as horses, carriages and drink. In this respect, compare him with some of those characters who are not imbued with quite so much life, such as James Morland. Do you think that the lack of metonymic association makes them relatively lifeless?

KEY QUOTATIONS: JOHN   A01

- John 'abducting' Catherine: 'Mr. Thorpe only laughed, smacked his whip, encouraged his horse, made odd noises, and drove on' (p. 84).
- Catherine starting to make her own judgements: 'she could not entirely repress a doubt, while she bore with the effusions of his endless conceit, of his being altogether completely agreeable' (p. 65).

MR AND MRS ALLEN

WHO ARE MR AND MRS ALLEN?

- The Allens are wealthy and childless landowners in Fullerton, where Catherine lives.
- They invite Catherine to accompany them to Bath.
- Mrs Allen and Mrs Thorpe are old schoolfriends.

THE HEROINE'S GUARDIAN

In **Gothic** and sentimental fictions, the heroine is frequently placed under the care of an irresponsible or actively malicious guardian. When Mrs Allen is first introduced this convention is parodied as the narrator, assuming a **satiric** stance, describes her in order that the reader may judge how 'her actions will hereafter tend to promote the general distress of the work' (p. 20). Initially, this appears very unlikely. Mrs Allen seems relatively harmless, and the narrator deals with her quite tolerantly, describing her as having 'a great deal of quiet, inactive good temper, and a trifling turn of mind' (p. 21). Her placid indifference, however, could have caused real damage to Catherine's reputation when she permits Catherine to go unchaperoned on a carriage drive, and she does not see that the Thorpes are unsuitable friends. At this point, Austen's satire sharpens, as the narrator comments on her 'vacancy of mind and incapacity for thinking' (p. 59). Mrs Allen's grip on matters of fashion may be admirable, but her grip on issues of morality and propriety is somewhat loose.

CHECK THE BOOK A03

The dangers of a young woman riding unchaperoned with a young man in a carriage are also at issue in *Emma* (1815) when Mr Elton becomes overly familiar with Emma Woodhouse. As Austen shows, the damage to a woman's reputation could be disastrous.

STUDY FOCUS: A WOMAN OF FASHION A02

Mrs Allen is defined above all by her preoccupation with fashion: 'Dress was her passion', as the narrator observes (p. 21). She judges others primarily on what they wear or own. Her moral confusion is indicated by her tendency to comment on such trivial matters when far more important issues are at stake. In Austen's works, such an obsession is a sign of a superficial nature and connected to a vulgar materialistic nature. Genuine, sincere characters are signalled by their lack of concern for their appearance: Catherine's declaration that she never minds dirt is consequently important (p. 79). Consider which other characters in the novel show an interest in fashion, such as Henry Tilney and Isabella. What does this show about their characters? Does it connect them with Mrs Allen, or is their interest in fashion quite different?

AVOIDING MRS ALLEN

Like Mr Bennet in *Pride and Prejudice* (1813), who avoids the endless chattering of his empty-headed wife by retiring to his study – consequently becoming an irresponsible parent too – Mr Allen seems to spend much of his time avoiding Mrs Allen. As soon as they arrive at the ball, he disappears into the more congenial male company to be found in the card room. While he is, therefore, more responsible than Mrs Allen – he checks out Henry Tilney, for example – his pronouncement on the impropriety of unchaperoned carriage rides comes much too late.

KEY QUOTATIONS: MR AND MRS ALLEN A01

- Mr Allen avoiding his wife: 'As for Mr. Allen, he repaired directly to the card-room, and left them to enjoy a mob by themselves' (p. 21).
- Mrs Allen's smug observance on her friend: 'the lace on Mrs. Thorpe's pelisse was not half so handsome as that on her own' (p. 31).

MRS THORPE AND FREDERICK TILNEY

WHO IS MRS THORPE?

- Mrs Thorpe is the impoverished widow of a lawyer from Putney.
- She is an old school friend of Mrs Allen.
- She is the mother of Isabella and John and has four other children.

THE INDULGENT MOTHER

Mrs Thorpe is a minor character characterised primarily by her indulgent love of and pride in her children. While Mrs Allen talks about clothes, Mrs Thorpe talks about her children. It is clear – and noted by Mrs Allen when she remarks on her friend's inferior lace – that Mrs Thorpe is not financially secure. Whether Mrs Thorpe is aware of the machinations of Isabella and John is not clear. She is certainly in a difficult position in having children to marry off, but she herself does not seem to plot in the manner of, for example, Mrs Bennet in *Pride and Prejudice* (1813).

WHO IS FREDERICK TILNEY?

- Frederick Tilney is the eldest son of General Tilney and the heir to the Tilney fortune.
- He is a captain in the 12th Light Dragoons (the army).
- He flirts with Isabella and causes the breaking of the engagement with James Morland.

ANOTHER VILLAIN

Captain Tilney is introduced in a manner similar to Mrs Allen. The **narrator satirically** suggests it unlikely that the apparently silly but harmless Mrs Allen will contribute to Catherine's misfortunes. With Captain Tilney she suggests it unlikely he will contribute to the downfall of Catherine since he has no interest in her at all. And yet, even more than Mrs Allen, Captain Tilney is a force of disruption in the novel, flirting with Isabella for his own amusement, with not the slightest intention of marrying her.

STUDY FOCUS: MATTERS OF INHERITANCE   A04

Primogeniture applied to landed property in Austen's time, and set down the law that a father must leave his property only to his eldest son. Established shortly after the Norman Conquest of Britain, primogeniture functioned to keep the estates of landowners intact. Under this system, daughters and younger sons were economically dependent on their father or elder brother. Austen often sets an undeserving first-born son against his more deserving young brother. Henry, following the usual practice, becomes a clergyman and has been provided for with the living of Woodston, but the bulk of the fortune will go to the disobedient and morally corrupt Captain Tilney. There are examples of laws of inheritance disadvantaging families in most of Austen's novels, including the Dashwoods in *Sense and Sensibility* (1811) and the Bennets in *Pride and Prejudice* (1813).

CHECK THE BOOK A03

The best-known rake or libertine in sentimental **romance** is Samuel Richardson's Lovelace in *Clarissa* (1748). Lovelace tricks the heroine Clarissa into eloping with him. She becomes his prisoner, and is kept in dubious lodgings, including a brothel. She continues to resist him, but he drugs and rapes her.

KEY QUOTATIONS: MRS THORPE AND FREDERICK   A01

- The friendship between Mrs Allen and Mrs Thorpe: 'Mrs. Thorpe talked chiefly of her children, and Mrs. Allen of her gowns' (p. 35).
- Mrs Thorpe on Isabella: 'we perfectly see into your heart. You have no disguise' (p. 130).
- Captain Tilney flirting with Isabella: 'If we have not hearts, we have eyes; and they give us torment enough' (p. 139).

THE MORLAND FAMILY

WHO ARE THE MORLANDS?

- Mr Morland is Catherine's father. His name is Richard and he is a clergyman and comfortably well off.
- Mrs Morland is Catherine's mother. Her time is taken up with looking after the youngest of her ten children.
- James is Catherine's brother. He is a friend of John Thorpe and he becomes engaged to Isabella Thorpe.

THE ABSENT FATHER

We learn very little about Mr Morland, apart from the fact that his name is Richard, he is a clergyman and comfortably well off. Indeed, he is strangely absent from the novel. We do not hear him speak: all parental advice comes from Mrs Morland. Even when Henry comes to Fullerton at the end, 'Mr Morland was from home' (p. 226). In this respect, Mr Morland is much in the style of the father of Gothic romance, who is usually dead and replaced by an autocratic father figure who terrorises the heroine.

STUDY FOCUS: THE SENSIBLE MOTHER A02

Mrs Morland is a plain-speaking woman who represents good sense, but also shows how good sense has its limitations. A kind and loving mother, she nevertheless lacks the imagination to understand the motivations of others. If her husband's wit is limited to the occasional use of a pun, her wit is limited to **proverbs** (p. 64). Popular phrases that express generally accepted truths, proverbs are by definition, unimaginative, reliant on oft-repeated folk wisdom rather than on wit and imagination. Can you envision Henry Tilney saying something like: 'A cat may look at a king' or 'A friend in need is a friend indeed'? When Catherine returns home from Northanger, Mrs Morland can only interpret her despondency as the result of being 'spoilt for home by great acquaintance' (p. 225). The idea that she might have fallen in love never crosses the Morlands' minds. Sense, as Austen shows throughout this novel, needs to be tempered with imagination, and imagination with sense.

THE DUPED BROTHER

James is studying to be a clergyman at Oxford, where he meets John Thorpe and, through John, Isabella. He is a good-hearted but not a handsome young man, and not particularly discerning in his friends. He considers John 'as good-natured a fellow as ever lived' (p. 49), and he is completely dazzled by the beautiful Isabella. Proving the old adage that love is blind, he is as incapable as Catherine of seeing through Isabella's manipulative strategies.

CHECK THE BOOK A04

For a discussion of Jane Austen's families, and in particular the interactions of the central characters with their families, see Jane Sturrock's *Jane Austen's Families* (2013).

KEY QUOTATIONS: THE MORLANDS A01

- The Morlands: 'plain matter-of-fact people, who seldom aimed at wit of any kind' (p. 64).
- The **irony** of James's view of Isabella: 'she has so much good sense, and is so thoroughly unaffected and amiable' (p. 49).

THEMES

CHECK THE BOOK A03

Another overly imaginative Austen heroine is the **eponymous protagonist** of *Emma* (1815). Like *Northanger Abbey*, this is a **Bildungsroman**, in which Emma causes many problems with her fanciful fictions until taught to see the error of her ways by her mentor-lover Mr Knightley.

EDUCATION

The process of education is central to *Northanger Abbey* as, indeed, it is to all Austen's novels. Catherine begins as a naive ingénue, and she has much to learn about people and society; she needs to be both educated and socialised. Who teaches her and what she learns have been a matter of some critical debate. Many critics would say Henry, the mentor-lover, playfully presides over Catherine's education. His **metaphor** about dancing and marriage, for example, points out at the very least the importance of being faithful to contracts of all kinds, and Catherine shows her understanding of this in her distress over the Thorpes causing her to renege on her appointment with the Tilneys. But others suggest Henry is a little too flattered by Catherine's adoration and, as when she dismisses the whole of Bath as unfit for a picture, perhaps she does not develop in herself through Henry but only echoes his beliefs and consequently appears absurd. In this reading, Catherine's main lessons come from experience, from learning to read others with more discrimination, and from coming to have faith in her own judgements.

STUDY FOCUS: HENRY AS MENTOR   A03

There are many scenes in which Henry profitably instructs Catherine in the novel, but his teaching culminates in the problematic 'Dear Miss Morland' speech (p. 186) that follows Catherine's investigation into Mrs Tilney's bedroom. For some critics Henry remains the voice of good sense; for others, his limitations are made clear. As Robert Miles argues in *Jane Austen* (2003), 'Henry has merely supplanted one kind of illusion (constructed out of the florid fantasies of **Gothic romance**) with another (the civil complacencies of Home Counties England)' (p. 42). Catherine, assuming Henry is always right, is consequently completely unprepared for the General's about-turn when he evicts her from the abbey. With Austen, anyone who risks such a dogmatic statement is sure to be shown wrong before long. Do you think Henry learns anything from his mistake?

KEY QUOTATIONS: EDUCATION   A01

- The **narrator** on the young Catherine: 'She never could learn or understand any thing before she was taught; and sometimes not even then' (p. 16).
- Henry and Catherine: '"Shall I tell you what you ought to say?"/ "If you please"' (p. 26).
- The narrator's **satiric** comment on love and **pedagogy**: 'Where people wish to attach, they should always be ignorant' (p. 106).
- Catherine makes up her own mind about the General: 'in suspecting General Tilney of either murdering or shutting up his wife, she had scarcely sinned against his character, or magnified his cruelty' (p. 230).

READING

Northanger Abbey is a novel about reading, full of references and allusions to other novels. It also has a **self-conscious narrator** who constantly draws attention to the fact that we are reading a work of fiction with such phrases as 'my heroine' (p. 217). Catherine's education, moreover, is an education in how to read properly: how to read texts but also how to read people and situations – she is completely oblivious to the developing relationship between James and Isabella, for example. In a sense, Catherine gets texts and people mixed up. She reads Isabella through the conventions of the sentimental romance. When Isabella professes her disinterest in money, the sentiment 'gave Catherine a most pleasing remembrance of all the heroines of her acquaintance' (p. 114). Her Gothic readings (and Henry's mock Gothic tale) lead her to act out a Gothic script with herself as heroine at Northanger, and she reads General Tilney through the conventions of the Gothic, seeing in him 'the air and attitude of a Montoni' (p. 176).

A key moment in the development of Catherine's reading skills is when she receives the letter in which Isabella attempts to persuade her to help in getting back James. For the first

time, Catherine recognises Isabella's duplicity (p. 203) and understands how she has been manipulated. Catherine is perhaps not quite right when she dismisses Isabella as a 'vain coquette' – the game she plays is far more serious than that – but at least she recognises Isabella's 'tricks' (p. 204).

GRADE BOOSTER **A01**

Northanger Abbey is a self-conscious fiction, in many ways a work of **metafiction**: as David Lodge defines it in *The Art of Fiction* (1993), 'fiction about fiction: novels and stories that call attention to their fictional status and their own compositional procedures' (p. 206).

STUDY FOCUS: LIFE AND FICTION   A03

Catherine is generally shown as naive in confusing life and fiction, and it leads her to be a flawed reader and a poor judge of character. Ultimately, however, Austen refuses any straightforward **dichotomy** between the two and shows them to be, in many ways, intricately entwined. In the scene on Beechen Cliff when Catherine and the Tilneys talk about history it is indeed Catherine who points out the connection, musing that a great deal of history must obviously be invented. Consider how this point becomes particularly important when the General evicts Catherine from Northanger Abbey.

KEY QUOTATIONS: READING

- An example of metafiction: 'my affair is widely different; I bring back my heroine to her home in solitude and disgrace; and no sweet elation of spirits can lead me into minuteness' (p. 217).
- Catherine reading Isabella's letter: 'Such a strain of shallow artifice could not impose even upon Catherine. Its inconsistencies, contradictions, and falsehood struck her from the very first' (p. 203).

IMAGINATION AND SENSE

A theme closely related to that of life and fiction is that of imagination and sense. Mrs Morland is the character most lacking in imagination and, in many ways, Catherine is initially much like her mother. This is partly why she is so taken in by such characters as Isabella. She tends to judge everyone's motivations according to what she would do, and this is a failure of the sympathetic imagination and is much like her mother's inability to recognise that Catherine is in love, and not just spoiled by her experiences at Northanger.

DEFENDING THE NOVEL

While *Northanger Abbey* is a **parody** of both the **Gothic** and sentimental **romance**, it is nevertheless also very much concerned to offer a defence of the novel, in particular in opposition to history, which was considered more appropriate reading for young girls, or those books of selections of canonical male authors of the kind that Catherine memorises when young. This too is a defence of the imagination, an assertion that there is much to be learned through reading fiction. Ironically, then, while novel reading may be dangerous when life is confused with fiction, at the same time novel reading is educational in that it can teach us about human nature (see also **Part Five: Literary Background**).

STUDY FOCUS: DOMESTIC TYRANNY   A04

While any attempt to define Jane Austen as a feminist should be carefully considered in light of the context of the times, feminist critics have nevertheless pointed out that she is concerned with the fate of women in a world in which they are so economically disadvantaged. Eleanor, as she points out to Catherine, is completely powerless. She is a virtual prisoner in the abbey, completely dependent upon, and under the power of, her father. Eleanor cannot be saved from this without Austen's wave of a magic wand at the end, when she provides Eleanor with a Prince Charming to take her away. In light of this domestic tyranny, it is worth going back to reread the description of Catherine's family situation at the start, paying particular attention to her father who 'was not in the least addicted to locking up his daughters' (p. 15). By the end of the novel, the improbable is shown to be not quite as improbable as we thought.

KEY QUOTATIONS: IMAGINATION AND SENSE

- The **narrator** on good sense: 'There was a great deal of good sense in all this; but there are some situations of the human mind in which good sense has very little power' (p. 223).
- The narrator on the novel: 'only some work in which the greatest powers of the mind are displayed, in which the most thorough knowledge of human nature, the happiest delineation of its varieties, the liveliest effusions of wit and humour are conveyed to the world in the best chosen language' (pp. 36–7).

CONSUMER CULTURE

Austen's novels are all set at a time when there was an expanding commercial sector and a growing consumer culture. (There is consequently perhaps some **irony** in the fact that of all authors in the late twentieth and early twenty-first centuries, excepting perhaps Shakespeare, Austen has had the greatest number of commodities and types of merchandise produced around her and her works.) Many of the characters in *Northanger Abbey* define themselves on the basis of their possessions, and judge others on the basis of theirs. Bath is presented in the novel as a consumer paradise, and actively promotes such values; a city full of tempting commodities, it is dependent upon its visitors who come to consume, not just to purchase ball gowns and hats and gloves and so on in the many shops, but also to consume food, water, concerts, plays and so on. It is a world of constant change, opportunity and excitement. Indeed, as Henry explains to Catherine, after staying eight or ten weeks in Bath, people 'go away at last because they can afford to stay no longer' (p. 76). Austen allows for no simple **dichotomies** in her settings, however, no false oppositions between the bustling modern commercial world of Bath and the antique rural world of Northanger. The abbey, a reflection of its materialistic owner, is similarly marked by commodities and consumption.

STUDY FOCUS: COURTSHIP AND MARRIAGE A03

Northanger Abbey, like all of Austen's novels, focuses on the theme of courtship and marriage. Austen's approach, however, is not like the romances with which we may be familiar today. While love is important, companionship is more so. There is little emphasis on sexual attraction – although it is not true to say that this is simply ignored by Austen – but relationships are based more on an attraction of minds than of bodies. Additionally, economics always underlie the marriages in the late eighteenth century: alliances are made between families, generally to consolidate wealth and land. Austen, however, usually rewards her female **protagonists** by 'marrying up'. For women in particular, marriage is a way of ensuring economic security. The marriage itself is of much less interest than what leads to it, and often quickly glossed over. If you are studying *Northanger Abbey* along with other Austen novels, it is worth comparing the 'rewards' given to the female protagonists, and what it is that Austen suggests makes them deserving. What, for example, connects Elizabeth marrying Darcy in *Pride and Prejudice* with Catherine marrying Henry in *Northanger Abbey*?

KEY QUOTATIONS: CONSUMER CULTURE

- Catherine on Bath: 'Oh! who can ever be tired of Bath?' (p. 76).
- The happy ending: 'Henry and Catherine were married, the bells rang and every body smiled' (pp. 234–5).

REVISION FOCUS: TASK 5 A04

How far do you agree with the statement below?

- The emerging consumer culture is shown to be a threat to the traditional social order in *Northanger Abbey*.

Try writing an opening paragraph for an essay based on this discussion point. Set out your argument clearly.

CHECK THE BOOK A04

Katherine Sobba Green's *The Courtship Novel*, 1740–1820 (1991) discusses the new ideal of companionate marriage, and shows how courtship novels of the time disrupted accepted ideas about how women should conduct themselves during courtship. Austen is one of many female novelists that she considers.

CRITICAL VIEWPOINT A04

In the eighteenth century, Ann Bermingham notes, 'the marriage market was a *real* market – that is an economic space for the exchange of goods and services, regulated by specific rules of decorum, brokered by institutions and protected by laws governing property … characterised by bargaining, negotiation and contractual agreements' (in Stephen Copley, ed., *The Politics of the Picturesque*, 1994, p. 97).

STRUCTURE

NARRATIVE STRUCTURE

Many early critics, following Mary Lascelles in her early but influential *Jane Austen and her Art* (1939), were preoccupied by what they saw as the novel's lack of **aesthetic unity**. In terms of its structure, they thought the two volumes did not hang together properly: that the comic **realism** and social focus in Bath were completely distinct from the supposedly inferior second part with its **parody** of **Gothic romance**. Later critics, however, have generally disagreed.

TRAVEL TO RETURN

Most of Austen's novels, as Barbara Hardy points out in *A Reading of Jane Austen* (1975), are structured around a movement emphasising an expanded social experience that will test and instruct the main characters (p. 107). In *Northanger Abbey*, this is demonstrated in the movement from the quiet village of Fullerton in Wiltshire to the busy social world of Bath, in which Catherine is inducted into society; then moving on to Northanger Abbey in Gloucestershire; back home to Fullerton with Catherine an 'altered' person; and concluding with the anticipation of Catherine being moved from father to husband and ensconced in another parsonage in another quiet village, this time Woodston.

STUDY FOCUS: OTHER STRUCTURAL CONNECTIONS A02

The two volumes seem well balanced. Modern bustling Bath in Volume One is set against ancient Northanger Abbey in Volume Two, but the two places are nevertheless closely connected: the abbey turns out to be just as modern, materialistic and consumer-driven as the town. Volume One focuses on the conventions of the sentimental romance, while Volume Two activates the conventions of the Gothic. In the first volume Isabella plays the major role in Catherine's education; John is the burlesque rake villain of sentimental romance while Isabella plays the sentimental heroine. In the second, Henry takes over the major role in Catherine's education, reversing the educational process of Volume One and correcting the mistakes produced by Isabella's influence. General Tilney appears as the Gothic villain, and Catherine initially plays the Gothic heroine only to learn her lesson and reap her rewards. You might also want to consider the degree to which so many of the conventions that are **satirised** in Volume One end up being exploited, in an updated form, in Volume Two.

FORM

NARRATIVE

THIRD-PERSON LIMITED NARRATION

The **third-person narrative** in *Northanger Abbey* is filtered primarily through Catherine. We see people and events through her eyes, and are given access to her thoughts and feelings in a way we are not with any other character. But Catherine's judgements are limited and often flawed, and the frequently **ironic** perspective of the **intrusive narrator** makes this clear. This is typical of Austen's narrative method: she tells the story from the point of view of a character while at the same time having the narrator comment upon and qualify that perspective with ironic and intrusive commentary.

THE INTRUSIVE NARRATOR

An intrusive narrator draws attention to the act of narrating and undermines the realistic illusion. Austen's narrator is very much in this style, speaking of 'my heroine', developing an easy relationship with the reader, and drawing attention not only to genre conventions but even to the material nature of the book when she notes that her readers will see in the 'tell-tale compression of the pages before them, that we are all hastening together to perfect felicity' (p. 233). This type of narrator is no longer popular, David Lodge observes in *The Art of Fiction* (1993), since it claims a kind of authority, a God-like omniscience, which our sceptical and relativistic age is reluctant to grant to anyone' (p. 10).

CHECK THE BOOK **A03**

Henry Fielding, author of such books as *Tom Jones* (1749), developed an ironic, detached and intrusive narrator, who reports and comments on the action, and is often seen to provide a model for Austen's narrative voice.

STUDY FOCUS: CHARACTERISING THE NARRATIVE VOICE **A02**

Austen's narrative voice may be easily recognisable, but how would you begin to describe it? For Terry Eagleton in *The English Novel* (2005), it is 'shrewd, amused, controlled, oblique, ironic, understated, though capable of sharpening from time to time into a rather more devastating dig' (p. 106). Notice how David Lodge uses similar terms when he defines Austen's voice in *The Art of Fiction* (1993) as 'lucid, measured, objective, with ironic implication concealed beneath the elegant velvet glove of the style' (p. 6). Try to summarise these main qualities, and identify examples of such writing.

GOTHIC

THE SHADOW SIDE OF ENLIGHTENMENT

Gothic fiction originated in the later eighteenth century, and the founding text is usually considered to be Horace Walpole's *The Castle of Otranto* (1764) – a book that, with its giant helmets and walking portraits, seems quite as comic to many readers today as *Northanger Abbey*. The **genre** was widely popularised by Ann Radcliffe, whose **Gothic romances** set the tone for the explosion of novels written in this style between 1790 and 1820. At the time, such novels as *The Mysteries of Udolpho* (1794) were not known as Gothic, however, but as 'romances', 'horrid novels' or 'the Radcliffe school'. It is this Radcliffean romance – sometimes called 'female Gothic' by critics today – with which Austen is primarily concerned: the focus is on beleaguered heroines, mysterious castles and aristocratic villains. The reader and the heroine experience psychological terror and suspense rather than

shocking physical horror, and all apparently supernatural events are explained away.

In reaction to these romances emerged the 'male Gothic' associated with such fictions as Matthew Lewis's *The Monk* (1796), which reworks Radcliffean conventions in a more violent form, focuses more on horror than terror, and is replete with gruesome descriptions of rape, murder, torture and with supernatural machinery – demons and ghosts – that are not explained away.

CHECK THE BOOK A03

Mary Shelley's *Frankenstein*, published in the same year as *Northanger Abbey* (1818), also exploits Gothic to comment upon an entirely secular world.

STUDY FOCUS: OLD AND NEW WORLDS   A04

The classic Gothic fictions of late-eighteenth-century Britain were set in past times and in distant countries, usually Catholic Europe. They functioned to define, by opposition, the values of English Protestantism and the **Enlightenment**: the championing of reason, privileging of science and rejection of superstition. While it may concern itself with scenes of transgression, Gothic is not, in itself, necessary transgressive. It may indeed be highly conservative. Gothic is concerned to define what is civilised and to reject what is seen as the primitive and monstrous 'other' that threatens the civilised self and society. What is monstrous is expelled in the interests of maintaining social and psychic stability. This is something to keep in mind when reading Henry's rebuke to Catherine outside his mother's bedroom.

According to Sue Chaplin in *Gothic Literature* (2011), Gothic is a mode of writing which 'responds in certain diverse yet recognisable ways to the conflicts and anxieties of its historical moment and that is characterised especially by its capacity to represent individual and societal traumas' (p. 4). With this in mind, do you think Austen can be said to exploit the Gothic as well as **parody** it?

CHECK THE BOOK A04

Elizabethan and Jacobean revenge dramas, such as John Webster's *The White Devil* (1612), exerted much influence on the figure of the Gothic villain.

THE HEROINE AND THE VILLAIN

In *The Mysteries of Udolpho*, Ann Radcliffe takes the sentimental heroine and places her in sixteenth-century Catholic Europe. Here she is in conflict with a villain representative of an aristocratic system of values that is shown to be both corrupt and dysfunctional. In *Northanger Abbey*, Austen also seems to be commenting on the corrupted nature of the ruling class. As Terry Eagleton observes in *The English Novel* (2005), 'it was on their culture, in the broad sense of values, standards, ideals and a fine quality of living, that the landowning classes had relied for so much of their authority' (p. 117). Austen does not object to the growth of a commodity culture; she objects, however, to the way in which it corrupts morals and manners and the way in which rampant individualism comes to undercut social responsibility, particularly the responsibilities of the ruling classes. The General is not in the least interested in helping others; he has what to Catherine seems like a 'whole parish to be at work within the inclosure' (p. 168) – and that word 'inclosure' inevitably echoes the idea of the enclosure system (see **Part Five: Historical Background**). These people work to produce luxuries like pineapples for him; they do not cultivate the ground for their own benefit.

IRONY

As David Lodge explains in *The Art of Fiction* (1993), **irony** is a **rhetorical** device that consists of 'saying the opposite of what you mean, or inviting an interpretation different from the surface meaning of your words' (p. 179). Irony questions the appearance of things, and since Austen is so often concerned with pointing out the reality behind appearances, it is appropriate that irony is prevalent in her work. She uses it for both comic and **satiric** purposes, exposing both delusions and errors. Unlike figures of speech like **metaphor** or **metonomy**, irony is not distinguishable by any peculiarity of verbal form. We understand irony purely through the act of interpretation.

PARODY

A parody is a work that comments on another work through satiric or ironic imitation. For Linda Hutcheon, in her influential *A Theory of Parody* (1985), parody plays ironically with multiple conventions, and combines creative expression with, most importantly, critical commentary. For Hutcheon, this approach to tradition results in what she calls a modern 'recoding' that establishes difference at the heart of similarity. Exhausted or redundant forms can consequently be rejuvenated and given new meaning or function. *Northanger Abbey*, then, can be seen to parody Gothic and sentimental romances, critiquing their conventions but also using them to comment upon such things as the position of women and the repressive responses to the threat of revolution in contemporary British society.

GRADE BOOSTER A01

Be aware of the difference between parody and **pastiche**. Pastiche is simply a jarring combination of different conventions, **tropes** and discourses. It aims for the absurd, and lacks the ulterior motives and satiric impulses of parody. Seth Graham-Smith's *Pride and Prejudice and Zombies* (2009), where modern zombie narratives are superimposed on Austen's story, exemplifies pastiche.

STUDY FOCUS: IDENTIFYING IRONY AND PARODY A01

- When Isabella says that 'there is nothing I would not do for those who are really my friends. I have no notion of loving people by halves, it is not my nature' (p. 39), how do we know the **narrator** is being ironic at her expense? We see the irony in the statement only because we understand Isabella and see the disparity between what she claims and what she is. Catherine, who has not, takes this as a literal statement.

- How do we read the narrator describing Mrs Allen so that 'the reader may be able to judge, in what manner her actions will hereafter tend to promote the general distress of the work, and how she will, probably, contribute to reduce poor Catherine to all the desperate wretchedness of which a last volume is capable—whether by her imprudence, vulgarity, or jealousy—whether by intercepting her letters, ruining her character, or turning her out of doors' (pp. 20–1). The parody here is of the irresponsible or actively malicious guardian of sentimental or Gothic romance. We see the difference, but we also recognise the connections. Mrs Allen will cause problems through her placid indifference and Catherine will indeed be turned out of doors, but the reasons are very much to do with Austen's world, and so the conventions assume new life.

CRITICAL VIEWPOINT A03

Austen's use of parody has received a great deal of critical attention. Tara Ghoshal Wallace, in an important article, '*Northanger Abbey* and the Limits of Parody' (*Studies in the Novel*, 20.3, 1988), suggests that the true subject of the parody is parody itself since she believes Henry's mockery of the conventions is responsible for what she describes as Catherine's subsequent hysteria.

CHECK THE BOOK **A01**

Students wishing to pursue the concept of the free indirect style in more detail will find Monika Fludernik's *Introduction to Narratology* (2009) full of helpful examples.

LANGUAGE

FREE INDIRECT DISCOURSE

Austen is particularly associated with the **free indirect style** of narrative, although she was by no means the first to exploit this. Generally speaking, the free indirect style allows the narrative voice to slip in and out of the consciousness of characters. Its effects, which can range from **satiric** exposure to sympathetic involvement, are best seen by comparing it with other ways of representing a character's speech or thoughts.

STUDY FOCUS: IDENTIFYING FREE INDIRECT DISCOURSE **A01**

- Direct speech is noted by quotation marks. For example, 'I have sometimes thought,' said Catherine, doubtingly, 'whether ladies do write so much better letters than gentlemen!' (p. 27).

- Indirect speech is reported speech without the quotation marks. For example, 'He thanked her for her fears, and said that he had quitted [Bath] for a week, on the very morning after his having had the pleasure of seeing her' (p. 53).

- Free indirect speech, rather than giving the words actually spoken by a character, gives words that reflect the way the character would think or speak. In *Northanger Abbey*, this simple form of free indirect speech is often put in quotation marks. For example, 'he supposed, however, "that she must have been used to much better sized apartments at Mr. Allen's"' (p. 158). Clearly, although put in quotation marks, it is not direct speech; if it were, he would have said 'I suppose, however, that you have been used to much better sized apartments at Mr. Allen's.'

- Free indirect speech becomes more interesting and complex when we are unsure if we are just reading the character's thoughts and views or if the **narrator**'s presence is also felt. Free indirect speech consequently introduces the possibility of **irony** or ambiguity. The challenge is to determine the status of the views presented. For example, consider Catherine musing on the black cabinet as so like that in Henry's story: 'though there could be nothing really in it, there was something whimsical, it was certainly a very remarkable coincidence!' (p. 159). We know this is Catherine because the signs of her curiosity and excitement at the possibility of **Gothic** adventures are all there. But is the narrator also in there winking at us, ironically suggesting that it is hardly a coincidence since Henry no doubt planted the cabinet in his story?

CHECK THE BOOK **A03**

Angela Carter frequently exploits free indirect style. Consider, for example, the moment the wolf arrives at the grandmother's house in 'The Company of Wolves'. It is difficult to know to whom we should attribute many of the statements in this passage, character or narrator, since the two tend to merge.

STUDY FOCUS: THE BEST CHOSEN LANGUAGE A02

In her defence of the novel, Austen describes it as a form that displays the 'greatest powers of the mind' and which conveys wit, humour and 'the most thorough knowledge of human nature' in *'the best chosen language'* (p. 37, emphasis added). On the basis of Austen's *Northanger Abbey*, how do you think Austen would define the 'best chosen language'?

To consider this question, let us turn to Norman Page in *The Language of Jane Austen* (1972). Page makes an important judgement about Austen's language that is worth considering in some detail. He observes that there is a 'conspicuous absence of words referring to physical perceptions, the world of shape and colour and sensuous response' and 'the recurrence of a relatively small number of frequently-used words, mainly epithets and abstract nouns indicating personal qualities, qualities, that is, of character and temperament rather than outward appearance'. Most of these words, he adds, 'seem to express the standards she deems desirable in human conduct and social relationships', although they may be used in terms of those who embody these standards or those who don't (p. 55).

Let's test that assessment. Choose a few characters – perhaps the three main female characters, Catherine, Isabella and Eleanor. Without looking in the book, try to give a physical description of each one, and then list a few words indicating their character and temperament. Which is the easier task? How much do you know about the appearance of these women (and remember no other Austen novel gives quite as much detail about dress and appearance as *Northanger Abbey*). There are some obvious details we remember – for example, Eleanor always wears white, but these memorable details have extra significance. (What colour is her hair? That's clearly not as important.) What about the words relating to character and temperament? Here are just a few that you can add to: taste, judgement, elegance, amiable, agreeable, wit, manners. Do you see how these often repeated words encapsulate all that is considered best in her world?

FIGURATIVE LANGUAGE

How often does Austen use such figures of speech as simile and **metaphor**? Many critics have argued that she is shy of figurative language, even distrusts it. In the *Art of Fiction* (1993), David Lodge suggests that her style 'claims authority partly by eschewing metaphor (metaphor being an essentially poetic figure of speech, at the opposite pole to reason and common sense)' (p. 7). Austen is more likely to exploit **metonymy**, a **rhetorical** device in which something is defined by what is associated with it. So, for example, consider how Isabella is defined by her connection with 'a pool of commerce' (p. 86), a card game. This is metonymy, not metaphor, at work.

REVISION FOCUS: TASK 6 A02

How far do you agree with the statement below?

● Austen tends to avoid the use of figurative language in *Northanger Abbey*.

Try writing an opening paragraph for an essay based on this discussion point. Set out your argument clearly.

CHECK THE BOOK A01

If the language of *Northanger Abbey* tells us much about what Austen values, so does the language of *Wuthering Heights* (1847) reveal what Emily Brontë values. It is worth comparing the scarcity of figurative language in Austen with what is sometimes almost a surfeit in Brontë.

CHECK THE BOOK   A01

Norman Page's *The Language of Jane Austen* (1972) is still one of the best books available on Austen and language.

LANGUAGE AND CHARACTER

One of the ways Austen individualises her characters is through their language. Isabella is probably the most obvious example. She has a tendency to **rhetorical** devices like **hyperbole**, with such phrases as 'I have an hundred things to say to you' (p. 38). There is the repetition of common intensifiers: Catherine is always 'my dearest' and Miss Andrews always the 'sweetest', while everything good is 'amazing'. There are also numerous exclamations, such as 'Psha, nonsense!' (p. 139). Isabella's language is that of the sentimental heroine, who is characterised above all by the intensity of her feelings. The repetitive, inaccurate and vague language of sentimentality is undercut, however, as it is usually repeatedly followed by rapid-fire chatter, and a sudden shift into comments about fashion or shopping. Isabella, above all, uses language to deceive: what she says is not what she means, because to say what she really she means would be to reveal her highly inappropriate ambition: to move up in the world through an advantageous marriage.

PRECISE ABOUT LANGUAGE

Henry teaches Catherine the importance of being precise in matters of language. On the one hand, we may find him rather pedantic, as Eleanor suggests when she defends Catherine's use of the word 'nice' by telling her brother he is 'more nice than wise' (p. 104). On the other hand, having seen Isabella's impoverished vocabulary, and the way in which she uses language to deceive, we may well agree with Henry about the importance of being 'nice' about language since words seem to have an intrinsic ability to deceive. Look, for example, at Henry playing with the confusion in understanding between Eleanor and Catherine about the shocking thing to come out of London. Notice how words can easily assume ambiguity: 'come out' can suggest something to be perpetrated or to be published while 'author' can be the perpetrator or the writer (pp. 107–8).

STUDY FOCUS: THE LANGUAGE OF THE TILNEYS   A02

In contrast to Isabella, Eleanor speaks politely and tactfully. Compare the way Isabella's language wildly veers between different registers with the balanced and simple speech of Eleanor, free of all slang, affectation and **hyperbole.** Henry's language, in contrast to the emotionalism of the Thorpes, relies on a lexicon of reason, something particularly notable in his rebuke to Catherine when he abjures her to 'consult', 'consider' and 'judge' (p. 186).

On the other hand, what do we make of Henry's use of the language of the **picturesque** in the episode on Beechen Cliff? If Isabella exploits the conventions of the sentimental **romance**, does Tilney's speech at this point show him also viewing life through a set of rhetorical lenses and, if so, is this all that much different from Isabella? Is it ever possible to see completely objectively, or does what we see always depend upon our education, society and culture?

PART FIVE: CONTEXTS AND CRITICAL DEBATES

HISTORICAL BACKGROUND

THE CONTEXT FOR THE NOVEL

While some critics have argued that Austen's works are apolitical and ahistorical, this is certainly not true of *Northanger Abbey*, which contains many references to the social, economic and political changes in her society. In the 'Advertisement' written in 1816, Austen asks the reader to remember that the work, while finished in 1803, was started and written much earlier, that 'during that period, places, manners, books, and opinions have undergone considerable changes' (p. 13). While some revisions were made and changes effected, in terms of social and historical context it is still overall a novel of the 1790s.

REACTIONARY POLITICS

These were years of social and political upheaval in England. The government, led by William Pitt, was caught up both in wars against France and in attempting to contain those inspired by the example of the French Revolution in 1789 who wanted to create a new social order within their own country, something known as English 'Jacobinism', that is, radical Republicanism. The increasing violence that came in the wake of the Revolution, from the September massacres of 1792 to the Reign of Terror in 1793–4, intensified fears about the possibility of similar revolt in England. The 1790s consequently saw the rise of reactionary tyranny, and the period 1794–9 in particular is often considered the most repressive in English history.

A REPRESSIVE SOCIETY

Leaders of radical groups were arrested and such legislation as the Seditious Meetings Act and the Treasonable Practices Act (both 1794) was passed to restrict the activities of dissidents. 'Habeas Corpus' (the right not to be imprisoned for an indefinite period without charge) was suspended, and this allowed for the imprisonment of political suspects without trial. A Newspaper Publication Act of 1799 attempted to control all criminal and seditious writings and censorship was the order of the day. Some critics have considered that General Tilney may be working for the government, as suggested when he says of his pamphlet reading, '*My* eyes will be blinding for the good of others' (p. 177). Voluntary associations of citizens emerged to report on seditious meetings and publications. Napoleon's expansionist policies and the wars with France kept Britain under the constant threat of invasion, and spies and informers were exploited by the government on an unprecedented scale.

THE TROPES OF REVOLUTION

The typical **tropes** of the **Gothic** – castle, prison, tyrant – were made surprisingly familiar and possible by the events of the French Revolution, and the eighteenth-century reader would have immediately understood the context for the discussion of riots caused by the misunderstanding between Catherine and Eleanor and the reference to spies in Henry's famous 'Dear Miss Morland' speech (p. 186) (see **Extended Commentary: Volume Two, Chapter 9, p. 186**).

GRADE BOOSTER A04

When discussing the social or historical context of a novel in your essay, always ensure it is not just presented as background material. You should make clear the relevance of the issues, linking them to the novel through direct textual analysis.

CHECK THE BOOK A04

Mary Shelley's *Frankenstein* (1818) is another Gothic novel of the time that shows the influence of the French Revolution. The monster himself has been seen as the emblem of the Revolution, something that initially has high aims, but is so abused that it turns destructive.

THE CHANGING LANDSCAPE

When Henry Tilney refers to 'the inclosure' in his lecture on the 'state of the nation' during the excursion to Beechen Cliff, he is referring to a movement that changed the landscape in the later eighteenth century. Numerous Enclosure Acts were passed during the years of the French wars, which meant the consolidation of common land into uniform plots: over 750,000 acres of countryside were enclosed in the second part of the eighteenth century. This was much to the advantage of the increasingly wealthy large landowners. It is only at this time that what we consider the 'characteristic' English fields and hedgerows appeared.

This enclosure of common lands led to the creation of a wage-labour force that was an essential stage in the development of modern capitalism. We see this in small scale in *Northanger Abbey* with the General's 'village of hot-houses' and numerous workers: a 'whole parish … at work within the inclosure' (p. 168) in Catherine's eyes. No longer working for themselves on common land, their labour serves only the economy of the abbey itself: the production of the luxury goods desired by the owner.

CONSUMER CULTURE

Since medieval times, the main centres for the exchange of goods had been local markets and fairs. This began to change in the eighteenth century, and the conduct of trade was gradually taken over by shopkeepers. The increasing affluence among the middle classes led to a much greater demand for goods, and the developments that resulted from the Industrial Revolution – such as better transport and an extensive system of roads – meant these demands could be easily filled. Shops increased not just in number and in the range of goods supplied but in specialisation. The result of all this was the development of what we call a consumer culture – a social and economic order based on the creation and fostering of the desire to purchase goods, and goods that are not necessary valued for their utility but relating more to the status they convey upon the purchaser. In Bath we see an example of how the desire for goods is created and fostered in the numerous shop windows. In the abbey we see the General's acquisitive nature and his association of his own status with the commodities he can display.

LITERARY BACKGROUND

NOVEL READING

The eighteenth century saw an unprecedented growth in the demand for the written word: there was a profusion of novels and an ever-increasing readership. *Northanger Abbey*, however, was written at a time when novel reading had come under serious scrutiny, and Austen is concerned to defend the novel from its detractors.

THE CIRCULATING LIBRARY

The largest market for fiction was not the individual because books were still very expensive to produce and therefore to buy. By 1800 most copies of novels were sold instead to the circulating libraries. These libraries allowed patrons who paid a membership fee to borrow their books. Novels were usually published in two or three volumes. A library would purchase a few copies and each volume being loaned out to individuals maximised the profit for the library. Inevitably, in catering to popular taste, the circulating libraries were full of sentimental and **Gothic** novels, leading to the Gothic being frequently described as the 'trash' of the circulating libraries. Much of this 'trash' was published by William Lane's Minerva Press. Minerva

had become synonymous with the Gothic novel in Jane Austen's time, and all the so-called Northanger canon – the novels on Isabella Thorpe's list (see p. 39) – were published by Minerva, with the exception of Francis Lathom's *Midnight Bell* (1798).

WOMEN AND THE NOVEL

The novel during the period of around 1780 to 1820 is very much associated with women, both as writers and readers, and it is in large part due to this that anxieties about novel reading characterised the age. Novels were repeatedly condemned in female conduct guidebooks and many female writers including Mary Shelley's mother, the feminist Mary Wollstonecraft, explore the dangers of fashionable novels, with Gothic and sentimental novels particularly singled out for condemnation.

Novels were considered, in the words of Dr Fordyce in his *Sermons to Young Women* (1765), a shameful violation of all decorum, encouraging woman to dwell on inappropriate scenes of pleasure and passion. Similarly, according to Hannah More in *Strictures on the Modern System of Female Education* (1799), the novel was 'one of the most universal as well as most pernicious sources of corruption among us' (Vol. 1, p. 191). Others more tolerantly argued that novel reading was dangerous because it raised unrealistic expectations about life in young women.

THE TRADITION OF THE FEMALE QUIXOTE

This led to a series of **parodic** novels in what is called the Female Quixote tradition, led by Charlotte Lennox's *The Female Quixote; or The Adventures of Arabella* (1752), which drew on the idea of Cervantes's *Don Quixote* (1615), in which the hero most famously mistakes a windmill for a giant and prepares to engage it in battle. Another heroine with romantic fantasies is farmer's daughter Cherry Wilkins in Eaton Stannard Barrett's *The Heroine: Adventures of a Fair Romance Reader* (1814). When she discovers a mysterious parchment and an old portrait in her father's desk she becomes convinced her father is actually an assassin planning to kill her and has him locked away as a lunatic. Calling herself the Lady Cherubina, Cherry takes off to discover her true parentage and causes three volumes worth of havoc, even at one point being committed to a lunatic asylum.

CONTEXT A04

Coleridge commented: 'as to the devotees of the circulating libraries, I dare not compliment their pass-time, or rather kill-time, with the name of reading. Call it rather a sort of beggarly day-dreaming during which the mind of the dreamer furnishes for itself nothing but laziness and a little mawkish sensibility' (*Biographia Literaria*, 1817).

CHECK THE BOOK A04

In *A Vindication of the Rights of Woman* (1792), Mary Wollstonecraft, asserts: 'Novels, music, poetry, and gallantry, all tend to make women the creatures of sensation and their character is thus formed in the mould of folly during the time they are acquiring accomplishments, the only improvement they are excited, by their status in society, to acquire' (Oxford Classics, 1975, p. 152).

CHECK THE BOOK A03

'Where Edward in the name of wonder, did you pick up this unmeaning Gibberish? You have been studying Novels I suspect' (from Jane Austen's **juvenilia**, *Love and Freindship*).

CONTEXT A04

The sentimental novel depicts scenes of extreme distress and emotion, and aims to elicit a correspondingly extreme emotional response from the reader. Henry Mackenzie's *The Man of Feeling* (1771), one of the most important of the British eighteenth-century sentimental novels, depicts the travels of the eponymous 'man of feeling', Harley, and his encounters with numerous distressed characters and situations.

CRITICAL VIEWPOINT A03

Janet Todd's *Sensibility: An Introduction* (1986) is a highly readable introduction to the sentimental novel. This kind of literature, Todd argues, was initially valuable in showing readers how to behave, how to express themselves, and how to respond to others. It was only later that it became more concerned with making its readers weep, and disintegrated into excessive emotionalism.

THE SENTIMENTAL NOVEL

Austen continually refers to, and **parodies**, the conventions of sentimental **romance**. The sentimental novel focuses on a heroine with a superabundance of refined and virtuous feeling: she is invariably beautiful, elegant, with many talents and a sympathetic appreciation of nature. When listing all the things Catherine is not, in order to demonstrate her unsuitability for the role of heroine, Austen's **narrator** expects us to recognise from our reading what she is speaking of; her **ironic** tone, which invites us to collude with her, suggests she assumes that we are well able to distinguish fiction from reality, and she does not expect the reader to regret Catherine's lack of these qualities.

The sentimental heroine is also, always, beset by many dangers. The plot revolves around her various distresses, such as the tyranny of a parent or her persecution by a hero villain, and concludes either with her death, presented in a highly sentimental manner, or, if she is luckier, her happy marriage to the man of her choice. Like Samuel Richardson's *Clarissa* (1747) it frequently exploits the letter or the journal, which can reveal the heroine's refined capacities for feeling more openly.

Austen rewrites many of the incidents found in popular sentimental novels. The **eponymous** heroine of Fanny Burney's *Evelina* (1778), for example, commits the crime of refusing to dance with one man and then accepting another, something close to social suicide at the time. Catherine goes through a moment of similar anxiety but makes the more sensible choice so that disaster is averted, although the description of her momentary suffering **satirically** draws upon the language of sentimentality. Similarly, the abduction by the villainous and unwanted suitor is cut down to size, replaced by an 'abduction' in which Catherine is forced on a tourist day trip, leading to comic incongruity between the discourse of the sentimental romance and the reality of events.

CRITICAL DEBATES

ORIGINAL RECEPTION

First published along with *Persuasion* after Jane Austen's death, *Northanger Abbey* did not suffer in contrast with the more mature work in the estimations of early reviewers, with most showing a decided preference for the earlier work. They commended the **realism** of *Northanger Abbey* in opposition to the torrent of sentimental and **Gothic** fictions, and admired in particular Austen's skill with character and her social observations about Bath.

Victorian commentators were divided. The historian T. B. Macaulay placed Austen only second to Shakespeare and – perhaps rather extravagantly – claimed *Northanger Abbey* was worth all of Dickens put together. G. H. Lewes similarly praised *Northanger Abbey*; in particular he praised the character of Catherine as a true flesh-and-blood young woman. Charlotte Brontë, on the other hand, was no fan of Austen, objecting to what she saw as the lack of passion in her works. Elizabeth Barrett Browning complained that Austen's characters lacked souls: 'The novels are perfect as far as they go', she added, 'Only they don't go far' (letter to John Ruskin, 5 November 1855). The idea that both Austen and her characters were passionless and prudish dominated mid-nineteenth-century thinking.

CHECK THE BOOK A04

Rudyard Kipling published a short story called 'The Janeites' (1926) in which an old soldier recalls how he joined a secret society of Jane Austen and offers his particular take on her works.

The first scholarly assessments of Austen were published in the last part of the nineteenth century. Her works was generally praised for the elegance of the writing, the realism of the fictional world, the humour and the morality. Most agreed, however, that Austen's work was limited in scope, focusing purely on domestic comedy. *Northanger Abbey* tended to be marginalised and placed with her **juvenilia**, also parodic and satiric, rather than with her mature novels.

JANE AND TWAIN

The publication of the *Memoirs of Jane Austen* (1870) by her nephew, the Reverend James Edward Austen-Leigh, turned attention to Austen herself. Austen-Leigh presented her as a respectable maiden aunt, an amateur writer who wrote masterpieces. In popularising Austen as a personality, the *Memoirs* also led to the rise of what have been called the 'Janeites'. While originally simply suggesting Austen enthusiasts, the term is now often used – not always fairly – in a rather derogatory manner to describe those whose interest in Jane Austen is seen as somehow lacking in scholarly value: distinguished by such things as costume balls, quizzes, reading clubs and conferences, study weekends and trips to places described in Austen's works. This kind of enthusiasm for Austen can be set against the numerous digs taken by such detractors as Mark Twain (see photo), perhaps Austen's most vocal, and certainly her wittiest, American critic.

CRITICAL VIEWPOINT A03

'Jane Austen? Why I go so far as to say that any library is a good library that does not contain a volume by Jane Austen. Even if it contains no other book' (Mark Twain, quoted in Robert Underwood Johnson, *Remembered Yesterdays*, 1923, p. 322).

CRITICAL VIEWPOINT A03

In *The Great Tradition* (1948), F. R. Leavis writes: 'Jane Austen, in fact, is the inaugurator of the great tradition of the English novel – and by "great tradition" I mean the tradition to which what is great in English fiction belongs' (p. 5).

CRITICAL VIEWPOINT A03

In *Jane Austen and Her Art* (1939), Mary Lascelles writes: 'There is weakness in the slight connexion between Catherine's fancied and her actual adventures at the climax of the story. The General's interference with her fortunes is neither a consequence of her foolish misconception of him … nor an amusing looking-glass version of it' (p. 64).

CHECK THE BOOK A03

Douglas H. Thomson's 'The Earliest Parodies of Gothic Literature' in *The Gothic World*, ed. Glennis Byron and Dale Townshend (2013), offers a survey of some Gothic parodies from 1788 to 1818 which can be usefully compared with *Northanger Abbey*.

TWENTIETH-CENTURY CRITICISM

AESTHETIC UNITY

Intellectual and travel writer Reginald Farrer published an introduction to Austen's fiction in the *Quarterly Review* of 1917. It identified Austen as a sharp critic of her society. This essay, along with the first scholarly edition of the novels, edited by R. W. Chapman and published in 1923, led to a revival of critical interest, and to the publication of Mary Lascelles's highly influential *Jane Austen and Her Art* (1939), the first full-scale historical and scholarly Austen study, and to F. R. Leavis placing Austen at the very forefront of his (now controversial) great tradition of English novelists.

Following Lascelles, early Austen critics were preoccupied by what they saw as *Northanger Abbey*'s lack of **aesthetic unity**. That is, they thought the two volumes did not hang together, and that the second, the **parody** of **Gothic romance**, was inferior to the first, the social comedy of Bath. The Gothic parody was seen to make no contribution to the advancement of the courtship plot. This position gradually came to be contested by such critics as Andrew Wright in *Jane Austen's Novels: A Study in Structure* (1953) who suggested this two-part structure was intended to show the inferiority of Gothic over **realism**. George Levine, on the other hand, later justifies the structure by arguing that the novel ultimately validates in Volume Two the principles it appears to parody and condemn in Volume One. In 'Translating the Monstrous: *Northanger Abbey*' (*Nineteenth-Century Fiction*, 30.3, 1975, pp. 335–50), Levine suggests that the monstrous Gothic villain is represented by General Tilney, and the true source of evil is shown to lie in such human frailties as greed.

GHOSTS OF THE GOTHIC

First prompted by the discovery in the early twentieth century that the 'Northanger canon' – those novels listed by Isabella Thorpe – actually existed, one enduring strand of interest has been Austen's sources in *Northanger Abbey*. This has ranged from such early works as Frank W. Bradbrook's *Jane Austen and Her Predecessors* (1966) to more contemporary scholarship such as Penny Gay's *Jane Austen and the Theatre* (2002). The main interest, however, has been in the influence of sentimental and Gothic romance, with Judith Wilt in *Ghosts of the Gothic: Austen, Eliot, and Lawrence* (1980) being one of the first to suggest that Austen makes the anxieties of everyday life just as important as the alarms of romance.

While the earliest of Austen's critics saw *Northanger Abbey* purely as a **satiric** and scornful attack on the Gothic and in particular Radcliffean Gothic, others began to argue that Austen never rejects the Gothic style but rather transforms it. Maria Jerinic's essay, 'In Defense of the Gothic: Rereading *Northanger Abbey*' (in Devoney Looser, ed., *Jane Austen and the Discourses of Feminism*, 1995), for example, argues against the position that Gothic is a bad influence. For Jerinic, reading is encouraged in the novel, and Catherine's reading of the Gothic does not create any delusions until Henry puts such ideas in her head with his mock Gothic story. The real danger, she suggests, lies not in women's reading of the Gothic, but in the way women accept men's interpretations of women's reading.

FEMINIST AUSTEN

While there have been many feminist readings of *Northanger Abbey*, critics have been divided over whether or not Austen is a conscious feminist in the tradition of Mary Wollstonecraft. Diane Hoeveler in 'Vindicating *Northanger Abbey*: Mary Wollstonecraft, Jane Austen, and Gothic Feminism', in Devoney Looser, ed., *Jane Austen and the Discourses of Feminism* (1995) notes the influence of Mary Wollstonecraft on Austen's depiction of the education of women. Hoeveler suggests Henry's role is to teach Catherine to think like a man. Claudia Johnson in *Jane Austen: Women, Politics and the Novel* (1988) offers a more historically based reading, seeing *Northanger Abbey* as a response to a politically repressive environment marked by fears of revolution, revolution in terms of both class and gender.

HISTORICAL AND POLITICAL CONTEXT

Most early Austen critics saw her as politically conservative and with little interest in the larger issues of her society. The main challenge to this position came with Marilyn Butler's *Jane Austen and the War of Ideas* (1975). Since Butler so convincingly located Austen's interests at the centre of intellectual debates following the French Revolution, few have attempted to challenge her political relevance. One of the earliest critics to offer a good historicist reading of *Northanger Abbey* was Robert Hopkins in 'General Tilney and the Affairs of State: The Political Gothic of *Northanger Abbey*' (*Philological Quarterly*, 57, 1978), which addresses the political context of the 1790s and suggests the General is part of the government's attempt to spy out sedition.

NORTHANGER ABBEY AND THE JUVENILIA

The relationship between *Northanger Abbey* and Austen's earlier works has been a matter of debate. Some critics identify the novel as connected more to the **juvenilia** – short parodic works that make fun of sentimental conventions; others see it more closely connected to her mature works. Juliet McMaster in *Jane Austen the Novelist: Past and Present* (1996), for example, sees *Northanger Abbey* as a kind of rewriting of 'The Beautiful Cassandra', with the self-indulgence transferred from the heroine to the villains.

AUSTEN COMPANIONS

There are now a large number of Jane Austen 'Companions' available, but it is necessary to distinguish carefully the academically sound works from those aimed at a more popular market; the latter, while often entertaining and frequently informative, may not be quite appropriate for consulting when writing your essays. (It is probably wise to avoid any contemporary 'critical' book that refers to 'Jane' rather than to 'Austen'.) The best of the scholarly Companions can offer useful introductions to Austen's work generally, and to various aspects of that work, including topics such as Money, Rank, Religion, Literary Genre and so on. Two very reliable Companions are *A Companion to Jane Austen*, ed. Claudia Johnson and Clara Tuite (2009) and *The Cambridge Companion to Jane Austen*, ed. Edward Copeland and Juliet McMaster (2011, revised edition). Another excellent book along similar lines is *Jane Austen in Context*, ed. Janet Todd (2005).

RECENT TRENDS

Since the beginning of this century, criticism has increasingly considered both the role of Austen in our modern culture and the role of late-eighteenth-century culture in Austen's works. With regard to the former, there is little specifically on *Northanger Abbey*, which, as yet, has not produced the kind of film and novel adaptations seen with Austen's other works. However, on Austen in modern culture generally, see in particular Suzanne Pucci's and James Thompson's *Jane Austen and Co.: Remaking the Past in Contemporary Culture* (2003) and Deirdre Lynch's *Janeites: Austen's Disciples and Devotees* (2000).

The other category, the role of eighteenth-century culture in Austen's works, includes some original and thought-provoking approaches to *Northanger Abbey*, most notably, perhaps, those essays dealing with the marketplace. This interest was already the focus of Ann Bermingham's 'The Picturesque and Ready-to-wear Femininity' (in *The Politics of the Picturesque*, ed. Stephen Copley and Peter Garside, 1994). More recent essays on this topic include Judith Wylie's '"Do you understand muslins, sir": Fashioning Gender in *Northanger Abbey*' (in Cynthia Kuyn and Cindy Carlson, eds, *Styling Texts: Dress and Fashion in Literature*, 2007); and Susan Zlotnick's 'From Involuntary Object to Voluntary Spy: Female Agency, Novels, and the Marketplace in *Northanger Abbey*' (*Studies in the Novel*, 41.3, 2009).

CHECK THE BOOK A04

The Juvenilia Press, founded by Juliet McMaster, has published a number of Jane Austen's juvenile parodies, including *Catherine or the Bower*, described as a significant transitional point in Austen's development as a writer.

CRITICAL VIEWPOINT A03

In *The Madwoman in the Attic* (1979), Sandra Gilbert and Susan Gubar write: 'Austen rewrites the gothic not because she disagrees with her sister novelists about the confinement of women, but because she believes women have been imprisoned more effectively by miseducation than by walls and more by financial dependency ... than by any verbal oath or warning' (p. 135).

CHECK THE BOOK A03

Val McDermid's contemporary reworking of *Northanger Abbey* for HarperFiction is forthcoming in 2014, and a film to be based on this adaption is already under discussion.

PART SIX: GRADE BOOSTER

ASSESSMENT FOCUS

WHAT ARE YOU BEING ASKED TO FOCUS ON?

The questions or tasks you are set will be based around the four **Assessment Objectives**, **AO1** to **AO4**.

You may get more marks for certain **AOs** than others depending on which unit you're working on. Check with your teacher if you are unsure.

WHAT DO THESE AOS ACTUALLY MEAN?

	ASSESSMENT OBJECTIVES	MEANING?
AO1	Articulate creative, informed and relevant responses to literary texts, using appropriate terminology and concepts, and coherent, accurate written expression.	You write about texts in accurate, clear and precise ways so that what you have to say is clear to the marker. You use literary terms (e.g. **protagonist**) or refer to concepts (e.g. **irony**) in relevant places.
AO2	Demonstrate detailed critical understanding in analysing the ways in which structure, form and language shape meanings in literary texts.	You show that you understand the specific techniques and methods used by the writer(s) to create the text (e.g. **free indirect style**, **authorial narrator**, etc.). You can explain clearly how these methods affect the meaning.
AO3	Explore connections and comparisons between different literary texts, informed by interpretations of other readers.	You are able to see relevant links between different texts. You are able to comment on how others (such as critics) view the text.
AO4	Demonstrate understanding of the significance and influence of the contexts in which literary texts are written and received.	You can explain how social, historical, political or personal backgrounds to the texts affected the writer and how the texts were read when they were first published and at different times since.

WHAT DOES THIS MEAN FOR YOUR REVISION?

Depending on the course you are following, you could be asked to:

- Respond to a general question about the text as a whole. For example:

Explore the ways in which Austen parodies Gothic romance in *Northanger Abbey*.

- Write about an aspect of *Northanger Abbey* which is also a feature of other texts you are studying. These questions may take the form of a challenging statement or quotation which you are invited to discuss. For example:

'Gothic literature challenges the status quo.' How far do you agree with this statement?

- Or you may have to focus on the particular similarities, links, contrasts and differences between this text and others. For example:

Discuss the ways in which illusion is set against reality in *Northanger Abbey* and another text you are studying.

TARGETING A HIGH GRADE

It is very important to understand the progression from a lower grade to a high grade. In all cases, it is not enough simply to mention some key points and references – instead, you should explore them in depth, drawing out what is interesting and relevant to the question or issue.

TYPICAL C GRADE FEATURES

	FEATURES	EXAMPLES
A01	You use critical vocabulary accurately, and your arguments make sense, are relevant and focus on the task. You show detailed knowledge of the text.	Austen's conclusion satirically exposes literary conventions as it briefly and dismissively summarises the marriage of Henry and Catherine: 'the bells rang and every body smiled' (p. 235).
A02	You can say how some specific aspects of form, structure and language shape meanings.	Modern bustling Bath in Volume One is set against ancient Northanger Abbey in Volume Two, but the abbey turns out to be just as modern, materialistic and consumer-driven as the town.
A03	You consider, in detail, the connections between texts, and also how interpretations of texts differ, with some relevant supporting references.	Both "Northanger Abbey" and "Jane Eyre" can be described as Bildungsromans, which are coming-of-age narratives that show the psychological development of the protagonists. While Jane, psychologically and economically, reaches a kind of independence by the end of the novel that makes her the equal of Rochester, it is not quite so clear that Catherine will ever move beyond being Henry's willing pupil.
A04	You can write about a range of contextual factors and make some specific and detailed links between these and the task or text.	The reference to the General looking over political pamphlets in Volume Two, Chapter 8 may well suggest he was part of the government's attempt to uncover anti-government views and plots in the wake of increasing fears of revolt in England following the French Revolution.

TYPICAL FEATURES OF AN A OR A* RESPONSE

	FEATURES	EXAMPLES
A01	You use appropriate critical vocabulary, technical terms and a clear, fluent style. Your arguments are well structured, coherent and always relevant, with a sharp focus on task.	The narrative voice is witty, opinionated, intrusive and, most importantly, self-conscious: that is, the narrator is clear and open from the start that this is a novel, and that she is the 'contriver', as she later describes herself (p. 217), of the fiction we read.
A02	You explore and analyse key aspects of form, structure and language and evaluate perceptively how they shape meanings.	When Catherine sees the key in the door and has a 'strange fancy to look into it' (p. 160), Austen brings to mind the story of Bluebeard and makes us, like Catherine, anticipate the revelation of some horror.
A03	You show a detailed and perceptive understanding of issues raised through connections between texts and can consider different interpretations with a sharp evaluation of their strengths and weaknesses. You have a range of excellent supportive references.	There is a striking contrast between representations of love in "Wuthering Heights" and "Northanger Abbey". On the one hand there is the unrelenting passion of Brontë's Heathcliff, who demands of his Catherine, 'Be with me always—take any form—drive me mad! only do not leave me in this abyss, where I cannot find you!' On the other there is Austen's narrator's confession that 'a persuasion of her partiality for him had been the only cause' of Henry giving his Catherine 'a serious thought'. It is hardly surprising that it is Brontë's lovers, and not Austen's, who have come to epitomise passion in the popular imagination.
A04	You show deep, detailed and relevant understanding(s) of how contextual factors link to the text or task.	"Northanger Abbey" is set at a time when there was an expanding commercial sector and a growing commodity culture. Bath, both a consumer paradise and an unofficial marriage market, embodies all the values of this culture, and Isabella, shopping for a husband who will provide her with the wealth and rank she desires, is the character most at home in this materialistic modern world.

HOW TO WRITE HIGH-QUALITY RESPONSES

The quality of your writing – how you express your ideas – is vital for getting a higher grade, and **AO1** and **AO2** are specifically about **how** you respond.

FIVE KEY AREAS

The quality of your responses can be broken down into **five** key areas.

1. THE STRUCTURE OF YOUR ANSWER/ESSAY

- First, get **straight to the point in your opening paragraph**. Use a sharp, direct first sentence that deals with a key aspect and then follow up with evidence or a detailed reference.
- **Put forward an argument or point of view** (you won't **always** be able to challenge or take issue with the essay question, but generally, where you can, you are more likely to write in an interesting way).
- **Signpost your ideas** with connectives and references, which help the essay flow.
- **Don't repeat points already made**, not even in the conclusion, unless you have something new to say that adds a further dimension.

TARGETING A HIGH GRADE

Consider the following essay question:

'Catherine has to learn to reject her Gothic fantasies.' How do you respond to this viewpoint?

Here's an example of an opening paragraph that gets straight to the point:

Henry's rebuke is often considered the key moment in Catherine's education: his correction of her 'blackest suspicions' (p. 176) about General Tilney leads to her subsequent dismissal of her Gothic fantasies and suggests she has learned her lesson. Soon after, however, when the General unceremoniously evicts Catherine from the abbey, it begins to seem that her instincts about the General, the result of her reading, are not quite as wrong as Henry likes to think.

Immediate focus on task and key words with example from text

2. USE OF TITLES, NAMES, ETC.

This is a simple, but important, tip to stay on the right side of the examiners.

- Make sure that you spell correctly the titles of the texts, chapters, names of authors and so on. Present them correctly, too, with double quotation marks and capitals as appropriate. For example, 'In Volume One of "Northanger Abbey" …
- Use the **full title**, unless there is a good reason not to (e.g. it's very long).
- Use the terms 'novel' or 'text' rather than 'book' or 'story'. If you use the word 'story', the examiner may think you mean the plot/action rather than the 'text' as a whole.

EXAMINER'S TIP ✓

Answer the question set, not the question you'd like to have been asked. Examiners say that often students will be set a question on one character (for example, Catherine) but end up writing almost as much about another (such as Henry). Or they write about one aspect from the question (for example, 'manners') but ignore another (such as 'morals'). **Stick to the question**, and answer **all parts of it**.

3. Effective Quotations

Do not 'bolt on' quotations to the points you make. You will get some marks for including them, but examiners will not find your writing very fluent.

The best quotations are:

- Relevant
- Not too long
- Integrated into your argument/sentence

Targeting a high grade

Here is an example of a quotation successfully embedded in a sentence:

The bewildered Catherine simply does not understand Isabella's innuendos and usually responds with 'a look of wondering ignorance' (p. 112).

Remember – quotations can also be a well-selected set of three or four single words or phrases. These can be easily embedded into a sentence to build a picture or explanation around your point. Or they can be longer quotations that are explored and picked apart.

GRADE BOOSTER A02

Make sure that you devote plenty of space to the close analysis of language. This will show that you have a deep understanding of the text, and the layers of meaning within it.

4. Techniques and Terminology

By all means mention literary terms, techniques, conventions or people (for example, **parody** or **metonymy** or 'Ann Radcliffe' – notice it is *not* Anne but Ann) **but** make sure that you:

- Understand what they mean
- Are able to link them to what you're saying
- Spell them correctly!

5. General Writing Skills

Try to write in a way that sounds professional and uses standard English. This does not mean that your writing will lack personality – just that it will be authoritative.

- Avoid colloquial or everyday expressions such as 'got', 'alright', 'ok' and so on.
- Use terms such as 'convey', 'suggest', 'imply', 'infer' to explain the writer's methods.
- Refer to 'we' when discussing the audience/reader.
- Avoid assertions and generalisations; don't just state a general point of view ('*Mrs Allen is obsessed with fashion so this makes her comical*'), but analyse closely, with clear evidence and textual detail.

Targeting a high grade

Note the professional approach in this example:

While Mrs Allen's obsession with fashion may seem to make her a comic character, it is perhaps not as 'harmless' (p. 21) as the narrator initially claims and actually functions to make some serious points about the materialism of the age. Her judgements of people are frequently and shallowly based on the evidence dress provides of wealth or class; she is, for example, impressed by Eleanor Tilney's pearls, but smugly scornful of the inferior lace on her friend Mrs Thorpe's pelisse.

EXAMINER'S TIP

Make sure you know how many marks are available for each **AO** in the task you are set. This can help you to divide up your time or decide how much attention to give each aspect.

QUESTIONS WITH STATEMENTS, QUOTATIONS OR VIEWPOINTS

One type of question you may come across includes a statement, quotation or viewpoint from another reader.

These questions ask you to respond to, or argue for/against, a specific point of view or critical interpretation.

For *Northanger Abbey* these questions will typically be like this:

- **In terms of structure, early critics thought the two volumes of *Northanger Abbey* did not hang together well. How would you argue against this position?**
- **Reading Gothic romance has taught Catherine to recognise evil. To what extent do you agree?**
- **To what extent do you agree that Henry educates Catherine?**
- **Discuss the view that Gothic is concerned with domestic tyranny.**

The key thing to remember is that you are being asked to **respond to a critical interpretation** of the text – in other words, to come up with **your own 'take'** on the idea or viewpoint in the task.

KEY SKILLS REQUIRED

SKILL	WHAT DOES THIS MEAN?	HOW DO I ACHIEVE THIS?
Consider different interpretations	There will be more than one way of looking at the given question. For example, critics might be divided about the extent to which the **Gothic** castle is a constraining space for the heroine.	• Show you have considered these different interpretations in your answer. For example: *When the critic Ellen Moers coined the term 'female Gothic' in 1976, she saw the castle as a source of freedom for the exploring heroine, and this is suggested, if parodically, in the way Catherine explores the secret spaces of Northanger. Other critics, however, see the castle as a confining space, and this is more clearly shown by the case of Eleanor, subjected to the domestic tyranny of her father.*
Write with a clear, personal voice	Your own 'take' on the question is made obvious to the marker. You are not just repeating other people's ideas, but offering what **you** think.	• Although you may mention different perspectives on the task, you settle on your own view. • Use language that shows careful, but confident, consideration. For example: *Although it has been said that ... I feel that ...*
Construct a coherent argument	The examiner or marker can follow your train of thought so that your own viewpoint is clear to him or her.	• Write in clear paragraphs that deal logically with different aspects of the question. • Support what you say with well-selected and relevant evidence. • Use a range of connectives to help 'signpost' your argument. For example: *Although the narrator asserts that Eleanor is given the 'home of her choice and the man of her choice' (p. 233), it is chance and not choice that results in the marriage. While men have the power to choose, this is not something granted to women in this world.*

ANSWERING A 'VIEWPOINT' QUESTION

Here is an example of a typical question on *Northanger Abbey*:

Discuss the view that *Northanger Abbey* ridicules Gothic romance.

STAGE 1: DECODE THE QUESTION

Underline/highlight the **key words**, and make sure you understand what the statement, quotation or viewpoint is saying. In this case:

Key words = **Discuss / Gothic romance / ridicule**

The viewpoint/idea expressed = **Austen ridicules Gothic romance**

STAGE 2: DECIDE WHAT YOUR VIEWPOINT IS

Examiners have stated that they tend to reward a strong view which is clearly put. Think about the question. Can you take issue with it? Disagreeing strongly can lead to higher marks, provided you have **genuine evidence** to support your point of view. Don't disagree just for the sake of it.

STAGE 3: DECIDE HOW TO STRUCTURE YOUR ANSWER

Pick out the key points you wish to make, and decide on the order in which you will present them. Keep this basic plan to hand while you write your response.

STAGE 4: WRITE YOUR RESPONSE

You could start by expanding on the statement or viewpoint expressed in the question.

- For example, in **paragraph 1**:

To ridicule something is to make it laughable and point out its inherent faults and failings, and this is what is suggested Austen does in "Northanger Abbey". It is certainly true that she could be said to ridicule Gothic romance through her satiric reproduction of its conventions. Her heroine Catherine, for example, fails to meet the standards for the Gothic heroine, her primary villain, General Tilney, is a materialistic modern version of a Radcliffean Montoni, and the Gothic abduction scene is cut down to size, as Catherine is forced on a tourist day trip. Comic incongruity is created between the discourse of the sentimental Gothic romance and the reality of people and events.

This could help by setting up the various ideas you will choose to explore, argue for/against, and so on. But do not just repeat what the question says or just say what you are going to do. Get straight to the point. For example:

However, it would be more accurate to say that Austen parodies, rather than simply ridicules, the Gothic. Parody has more of a function: it plays ironically with conventions in order to combine new creative expression with critical commentary. The forms of persecution and entrapment are not just reproduced in comic form, but also, more seriously, shown to exist still in an updated form within the modern world. The General may not precisely be a Radcliffean Montoni, but he is an unpleasant man, driven by greed, and he subjects Catherine to some very real dangers when he evicts her from Northanger.

Then, proceed to set out the different arguments or critical perspectives, including your own. This might be done by dealing with specific aspects or elements of the novel, one by one. Consider giving 1–2 paragraphs to explore each aspect in turn. Discuss the strengths and weaknesses in each particular point of view. For example:

- **Paragraph 2:** first aspect:

*To answer whether this interpretation is valid, we need to **first of all** look at ...*

***It is clear from this** that... /a **strength** of this argument is ...*

*However, I believe this suggests that .../a **weakness** in this argument is ...*

- **Paragraph 3:** a new focus or aspect:

Turning our attention to the critical idea that *... it could be said that ...*

- **Paragraphs 4, 5, etc., onwards:** develop the argument, building a convincing set of points:

Furthermore, *if we look at ...*

- **Last paragraph:** end with a clear statement of your view, without simply listing all the points you have made.

EXAMINER'S TIP

You should comment concisely, professionally and thoughtfully and present a range of viewpoints. Try using modal verbs such as 'could', 'might', 'may' to clarify your own interpretation. For additional help on **Using critical interpretations and perspectives**, see pages 106 and 107.

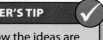

EXAMINER'S TIP

Note how the ideas are clearly signposted through a range of connectives and linking phrases, such as 'However' and 'Turning our attention to ...'.

COMPARING *NORTHANGER ABBEY* WITH OTHER TEXTS

As part of your assessment, you may have to compare *Northanger Abbey* with, or link it to, other texts that you have studied. These may be other novels, plays or even poetry. You may also have to link or draw in references from texts written by critics. For example:

> **Compare the presentation of curiosity in** *Northanger Abbey* **and other text(s) you have studied.**

THE TASK

Your task is likely to be on a method, issue, viewpoint or key aspect that is common to *Northanger Abbey* and the other text(s), so you will need to:

> **Evaluate the issue** or statement and have an **open-minded approach**. The best answers suggest meaning**s** and interpretation**s** (plural):
> - What do you understand by the question? Is this theme more important in one text than in another? Why? How?
> - What are the different ways that this question or aspect can be read or viewed?
> - Can you challenge the viewpoint, if there is one? If so, what evidence is there? How can you present it in a thoughtful, reflective way?

> **Express original or creative approaches** fluently:
> - This isn't about coming up with entirely new ideas, but you need to show that you're actively engaged with thinking about the question and are not just reproducing random facts and information you have learned.
> - **Synthesise** your ideas – pull ideas and points together to create something fresh.
> - This is a linking/comparison response, so ensure that you guide your reader through your ideas logically, clearly and with professional language.

> **Know what to compare/contrast: form, structure** and **language** will **always** be central to your response, even where you also have to write about characters, contexts or culture.
> - Think about standard versus more unconventional **narration** (for example, use of flashback, **foreshadowing**, disrupted time or narrative voice which leads to dislocation or difficulty in reading).
> - Consider different characteristic uses of language: length of sentences, formal/informal style, dialect, accent, balance of dialogue and narration; the difference between forms, if appropriate (for example, prose treatment of an idea and a play).
> - Look at a variety of **symbols**, **images**, **motifs** (how they represent concerns of author/time; what they are and how and where they appear; how they link to critical perspectives; their purposes, effects and impact on the novel).
> - Consider aspects of **genres** (to what extent do Austen and the author(s) of the other work(s) conform to/challenge/subvert particular genres or styles of writing?).

EXAMINER'S TIP ✓

Be sure to give due weight to each text – if there are two texts, this would normally mean giving them equal attention (but check the exact requirements of your task). Where required or suggested by the course you are following, you could try moving fluently between the texts in each paragraph, as an alternative to treating texts separately. This approach can be impressive and will ensure that comparison is central to your response.

WRITING YOUR RESPONSE

The depth and extent of your answer will depend on how much you have to write, but the key will be to **explore in detail**, and **link between ideas and texts**. Let's use the example from page 102:

> **Compare the presentation of curiosity in** *Northanger Abbey* **and other text(s) you have studied.**

INTRODUCTION TO YOUR RESPONSE

- In relation to the question above, you might briefly begin with the standard **trope** of the curious heroine, noting it goes back to the stories of Pandora and Eve, and becomes particularly associated with the tale of Bluebeard.

- You could begin with a powerful quotation that you use to launch into your response. For example:

> *'The key was in the door' and, like numerous heroines from Pandora and Eve to Bluebeard's wife, Catherine Morland is prompted by insatiable curiosity and 'had a strange fancy to look into' the cabinet (p. 160). While Catherine is destined to disappointment, the heroine of Angela Carter's "The Bloody Chamber"…*

MAIN BODY OF YOUR RESPONSE

- **Point 1**: start with the dramatic presentation of curiosity in *Northanger Abbey* and what this tells us about the novel's main concerns. What is your view? Are the uses of curiosity similar in the other text(s)? Are there any relevant critical viewpoints that you know about? Are there contextual or cultural factors to consider?

- **Point 2**: now cover a new treatment or aspect through comparison or contrast of this theme in your other text(s). How is this treatment or aspect presented **differently or similarly** by the writer(s) in the language, form, structures used? Why was this done in this way? How does it reflect the writers' interests? What do the critics say? Are there contextual or cultural factors to consider?

- **Points 3, 4, 5, etc.**: address a range of other factors and aspects, for example the role played by characters apart from the **protagonists either** within *Northanger Abbey* or in both *Northanger Abbey* and another text. What different ways do you respond to these (with more empathy, greater criticism, less interest) – and why? For example:

> *In "Northanger Abbey", the role of Bluebeard is played by General Tilney, the domestic tyrant Catherine suspects to have either locked up or murdered his wife. Catherine is wrong, but his materialistic and tyrannical nature makes Tilney still a much less empathetic figure than Rochester who, having literally locked his wife up in the attic, assumes the role of Bluebeard in "Jane Eyre".*

CONCLUSION

- Synthesise elements of what you have said into a final paragraph that fluently, succinctly and inventively leaves the reader/examiner with the sense that you have engaged with this task and the texts. For example:

> *Ultimately, while curiosity is shown to be dangerous, it is also shown to be the essential element in each heroine's development of an independent identity. Because she questions, because she refuses the limitations of the role set out for her and seeks the truth for herself, each heroine avoids ending up as a victim of domestic tyranny and is instead rewarded with domestic bliss.*

EXAMINER'S TIP ✓

Be creative with your conclusion! It's the last thing the examiner will read and your chance to make your mark.

RESPONDING TO A GENERAL QUESTION ABOUT THE WHOLE TEXT

You may also be asked to write about a specific aspect of *Northanger Abbey* – but as it relates to the **whole text**. For example:

> **Explore the dramatic use of setting in *Northanger Abbey*.**

This means you should:

- Focus on *all the main settings*, including Bath, Northanger and Woodston.
- Explain their **dramatic use** – *how* they are used in terms of structure, character and furthering ideas or themes.
- Look at aspects of the **whole novel**, not just one part.

STRUCTURING YOUR RESPONSE

You need a clear, logical plan, as for all tasks that you do. It is impossible to write about every section or part of the text, so you will need to:

- Quickly note 5–6 key points or aspects to build your essay around, e.g.

  Point a *Fullerton, Catherine's home, is a small village we learn little about.*
  Point b *Woodston is an idealised Fullerton, bringing Catherine full-circle home.*
  Point c *Northanger is structurally set in contrast to Bath through Catherine's expectations, but is just as modern and materialistic. General Tilney embodies this materialism.*
  Point d *Bath is associated with the consumer world and is a marriage market. Isabella embodies its values.*
  Point e *Setting functions to show Catherine's literal and metaphorical journeys.*

- Then decide the most effective or logical order. For example, **point e**, then **a**, **d**, **c**, **b**, etc.

You could begin with your key or main idea, with supporting evidence/references, followed by your further points (perhaps two paragraphs for each). For example:

Paragraph 1: first key point: *Setting in "Northanger Abbey" functions primarily to show Catherine's development, not simply her journey from one place to another but also her metaphorical journey from child to mature adult.*

Paragraph 2: expand out, link into other areas: *Catherine is brought up in a small village; she has a sheltered childhood, making her naive in many ways, and setting her up as someone who needs to be educated in the ways of the world.*

Paragraph 3: change direction, introduce new aspect/point: *Her trip to Bath with the Allens introduces Catherine to a consumer-driven world and to intrigue and duplicity, things embodied in the character of Isabella.*

And so on.

- For your **conclusion**, use a compelling way to finish, perhaps repeating some or all of the key words from the question. For example, either:

End with your final point, but **add a last clause** which makes it clear what you think is key to the question:

Ending with the anticipation of Catherine going to live in Woodston, Austen shows her heroine has left behind all her Gothic imaginings; the Abbey is of no further interest, and what she looks forward to instead is a pretty village and a comfortable parsonage.

Or end with a **new quotation** and/or an **aspect** that's **slightly different** from your main point:

Ending with the anticipation of Catherine going to live in Woodston, Austen shows her heroine has learned to value what she initially left behind and is consequently rewarded with the 'unpretending comfort of a well-connected Parsonage, something like Fullerton but better' (p. 199).

WRITING ABOUT CONTEXTS

Assessment Objective 4 asks you to 'demonstrate understanding of the significance and influence of the contexts in which literary texts are written and received ...'. This can mean:

- How the events, settings, politics and so on **of the time when the text was written** influenced the writer or help us to understand the novel's themes or concerns. For example, how do anxieties over novel reading at the time impact upon Austen's text?

or

- How events, settings, politics and so on **of the time when the text is read or seen** influence how it is understood. For example, do we as modern readers understand the political references to spies, riot and revolution as easily as Austen's contemporaries?

THE CONTEXT FOR *NORTHANGER ABBEY*

You might find the following table of suggested examples helpful for thinking about how particular aspects of the time contribute to our understanding of the novel and its themes. These are just examples – can you think of any others?

POLITICAL	LITERARY	PHILOSOPHICAL
French Revolution	Sentimental **romance** **Gothic** romance	Imagination and reason

SCIENTIFIC	CULTURAL	SOCIAL
Improvement in transport systems	Tourism and the **picturesque**	Morals and manners Marriage contract

TARGETING A HIGH GRADE · AO4

Remember that the extent to which you write about these contexts will be determined by the marks available. Some questions or tasks may have very few marks allocated for **AO4**, but where you do have to refer to context the key thing is not to 'bolt on' your comments, or write a long, separate chunk of text on context and then 'go back' to the novel. For example:

Don't just write:

The late eighteenth century was a time of social and political upheaval in England. The government, led by William Pitt, was caught up in wars against France, and Napoleon's expansionist policies kept Britain under the constant threat of invasion. Spies and informers were exploited by the government on a never before seen scale. In the wake of the French Revolution, there were also intensified fears about the possibility of similar revolt in England. The 1790s consequently saw the rise of reactionary tyranny, and the period 1794–9 in particular is often considered the most repressive in English history. General Tilney is sometimes seen as contributing to the state's attempts to seek out and eliminate seditious publications.

Do write:

While Austen is sometimes considered ahistorical and apolitical, this is certainly not true of "Northanger Abbey". Austen's first readers would have found evidence of the government's repressive policies in the wake of the French Revolution throughout the novel. When General Tilney is seen poring over pamphlets well into the night, for example, Austen suggests he may well be part of the state's programme to seek out and eliminate anti-government publications.

EXAMINER'S TIP

Remember that linking the historical, literary or social context to the novel is key to achieving the best marks for **AO4**.

USING CRITICAL INTERPRETATIONS AND PERSPECTIVES

THE 'MEANING' OF A TEXT

There are many viewpoints and perspectives on the 'meaning' of *Northanger Abbey*, and examiners will be looking for evidence that you have considered a range of these. Broadly speaking, these different interpretations might relate to the following considerations:

1. CHARACTER

What **sort/type** of person Catherine – or another character – is:

- Is the character an 'archetype' (a specific type of character with common features)? Catherine has been described as an ingénue, for example, a naive and innocent stock character.

- Does the character personify, **symbolise** or represent a specific idea or **trope** (for example, the dangers of imagination as opposed to reason, the problems of innocence as opposed to experience)?

- Is the character modern, universal, of his/her time, historically accurate, etc.? For example, how is Catherine like or not like the **Gothic** heroines of Ann Radcliffe, or how is she like or unlike later Victorian heroines such as Jane Eyre or Catherine of *Wuthering Heights* or the more recent heroine of Angela Carter's title story from *The Bloody Chamber*?

CRITICAL VIEWPOINT A03

'Continuously sensitising us to the mediating properties of gothic conventions, Austen provides the readers of her own as well as Radcliffe's novels with the distance necessary to see the dark and despotic side of the familiar and to experience it as "strange" rather than as proper and inevitable' (Claudia Johnson, *Jane Austen: Women, Politics and the Novel*, 1988, p. 48).

2. IDEAS AND ISSUES

What the novel tells us about **particular ideas or issues** and how we can interpret these. For example:

- Consumer culture
- Gothic and tyranny
- The dangers of imagination and the limitations of reason
- Manners and morals

3. LINKS AND CONTEXTS

To what extent the novel **links with, follows or pre-echoes** other texts and/or ideas. For example:

- What is the novel's influence culturally, historically and socially? Do we see echoes of the characters or **genre** in other texts? How is Catherine like or not like a Gothic heroine, and why? Does the novel share features with other **Bildungsromans** like *Jane Eyre*?

- How does its language link to other texts or modes, such as Carter's revisionist fairy tales or modern romantic fiction?

4. DRAMATIC STRUCTURE

How the novel is **constructed** and how Austen **makes** her narrative:

- Does the structure contribute to meaning?
- What is the function of specific events, characters, setting, etc. in relation to narrative?
- What are the specific moments of tension, conflict, crisis and denouement – and do we agree on what they are?

5. READER RESPONSE

How the novel **works on a reader**, and whether this changes over time and in different contexts:

- Do we empathise with, feel distance from, judge and/or evaluate events and characters?

6. CRITICAL REACTION

- How do different readers view the novel? Consider, for example, nineteenth- and twenty-first-century readers, and feminist critics as opposed to structuralist critics.

WRITING ABOUT CRITICAL PERSPECTIVES

The important thing to remember is that **you** are a critic too. Your job is to evaluate what a critic or school of criticism says about the elements above, and make your own conclusions.

In essence, you need to: **consider** the views of others, **synthesise** them, then decide on **your perspective**. For example:

EXPLAIN THE VIEWPOINTS

Critical view A about Henry as Catherine's teacher:

> *Early critics such as Howard S. Babb saw Henry as Catherine's teacher: in Volume One he teaches her about the world; in Volume Two he teaches her about herself.*

Critical view B about Henry as Catherine's teacher:

> *Later feminist critics like Susan Morgan, however, see Catherine learning to make her own judgements and trusting her own instincts, rather than relying on Henry's lessons.*

THEN SYNTHESISE AND ADD YOUR PERSPECTIVE

Synthesise these views whilst adding your own:

> *The idea of the mentor-lover can be found throughout Austen's novels, and Henry seems to fit in with this tradition in many ways, particularly in the way he teaches Catherine about social conventions in Volume One. In Volume Two, however, as Catherine begins to learn to make her own judgements and to trust her own instincts, Henry's rational approach to the world comes to seem a little too dogmatic. He is quite wrong, for example, when he suggests that crimes and atrocities could not be committed in a modern England. Henry may be Catherine's teacher, but there are things he too needs to learn.*

GRADE BOOSTER A03

Make sure you have a good sense of how critical interpretations of the novel have changed over the years, and bear in mind that views of texts can change as values change.

TARGETING A HIGH GRADE

Ensure you have thoroughly explored the different types of criticism written about *Northanger Abbey*. Critical interpretations of a novel can range from reviews and comments made at the time it was published to modern critical analysis. Remember that views of texts change over time, and that critics do not write in a vacuum. For example, the mid-twentieth-century obsession with the lack of 'aesthetic unity' in *Northanger Abbey* is very much the product of the strong influence of the New Criticism popular at the time, a school of thought which valued aesthetic unity above all. Similarly, the growth of interest in Austen as a feminist in the late 1970s and 1980s is inevitably linked to the rise of second-wave feminism at the time.

ANNOTATED SAMPLE ANSWERS

Below are extracts from two sample answers to the same question at different grades. Bear in mind that these are examples only, covering all four Assessment Objectives – you will need to check the type of question and the weightings given for the four Assessment Objectives when writing your coursework essay or practising for your exam.

> Question: 'Jane Austen uses Gothic tropes in *Northanger Abbey* only to ridicule them.' How far do you agree with this view?

CANDIDATE 1

The most famous examples of Gothic fiction were written by Ann Radcliffe, and these kinds of novels focus on a heroine who is removed from the safety of her home, often because of the death of her parents, and goes on some journey in which she is imprisoned or threatened in ruined castles or abbeys in the Alps or Pyrenees. Instead of being persecuted by the cruel father and the libertine, the Gothic heroine is threatened by aristocratic tyrants or banditti who are after their money or their virtue. In "Northanger Abbey", Jane Austen uses Gothic tropes not just to ridicule the Gothic, but also to create effects and to show that the General is a villain.

A04 While this is useful literary context, it is always better to start your essay by immediately engaging with the text you are writing about, rather than contextual issues

A02 Quite a good statement of your position but what are these effects? Be more specific: tone, dramatic tension, etc.

Henry tells Catherine a mock Gothic story on the journey to Northanger Abbey. This makes Catherine expect danger but also the reader. This is all part of the way in which Austen creates dramatic tension. Catherine's expectation of Northanger Abbey is also added to by her previous reading of Gothic romance. The abbey is disappointing to her, since there is nothing Gothic about it. After this, each time Catherine expects something Gothic to happen, she is disappointed and the reader is invited to laugh at her.

A02 Dramatic tension is important, but analyse how it is created with attention to detail

A02 There are no quotations from the text in any of the first three paragraphs – examples must be used as evidence for ideas and for the discussion of language

A02 This whole paragraph is much too general and a bit confused – too many points are brought in and not developed

The use of Gothic tropes in Volume Two also creates a contrast in tone with the social comedy in Bath in Volume One. There, Gothic fiction is just something fashionable that Isabella and Catherine read. For example, Catherine reads Ann Radcliffe's "The Mysteries of Udolpho" and is particularly caught up in the mystery of the black veil which she enjoys discussing with her friend. Once at Northanger, however, Gothic becomes something Catherine is living rather than reading, and the tone of the novel consequently changes. Catherine becomes the main character in her own Gothic drama. Life and fiction become confused.

A01 Another good concept to consider

A03 Useful to connect with this other text, but explain relevance of black veil to your argument

A02 Excellent point, but effect of this could be discussed

Some critics would say that there is actually no overall difference in tone between the two parts because Austen's voice as the narrator is so obvious. For example, when Catherine spots 'an immense heavy chest' that makes her curious, Austen describes Catherine's thoughts through Gothic tropes: the handles have been broken by 'some

A04 It would be much better to name a specific critic.

strange violence' and the 'mysterious cypher' on the lid. But the reader is not caught up in the mystery as Catherine is because of that narrative voice that, in describing the chest as an 'object so well calculated to interest and alarm', reveals to us that Catherine has been set up by Henry, who mentioned the chest in his earlier mock Gothic tale.

AO2 Good quotation, but you could explain the point a little more clearly with an emphasis on 'calculated'

AO1 More of these connectives would be helpful in showing a development of argument

When Catherine is about to be evicted from Northanger, however, the narrative voice is less opinionated. Austen presents Catherine as a figure of sympathy, not satire. This is shown in the contrast between her earlier Gothic fears and how she faces the 'actual and natural evil'. The idea of evil takes on different meanings. The abbey no longer frightens her, and she is unaffected by the 'strange and sudden noises throughout the house', she is now 'without curiosity or terror'.

AO2 Good quotations to use, but analyse language more

Gothic tropes may be ridiculed at first, but in the end they show that the boundary between fiction and reality is actually not as well defined as Henry suggests in his rebuke outside his mother's bedroom. We get a clue that this will happen in Henry's send-up of Eleanor's and Catherine's misunderstanding over the 'something very shocking [that] will soon come out in London'. While Henry laughs at his sister's extreme fear of such horrors as 'a mob of three thousand men assembling in St. George's Fields', we as readers know that Henry's description echoes real events: London has suffered such 'horrors'. Fiction and reality are not always completely distinct.

AO1 Good to engage with this theme, but you need to prepare for this earlier and explain how it is part of your argument

AO4 Good use of contextual detail but description is rather vague

When Catherine lets her imagination run wild in Gothic terms when she imagines the General has either locked up or murdered his wife, she is not completely wrong. When he orders that Catherine should be evicted from the abbey, humiliated and sent home alone on a dangerous journey, it begins to seem that Gothic villainy is alive and well in the midland counties of England. Catherine's knowledge of the Gothic helps her to see that the General is a modern kind of tyrant: he has tyrannised his wife and his daughter and he is cruel to Catherine. No matter what Henry says, Catherine sees something in his 'air and attitude' that is like the Gothic villain Montoni, and she is proven to be right.

AO4 Appropriate literary reference but could be further developed

GRADE C

Comment

While this answer engages with many important points, it does not develop them all in enough detail. Nor does it manage to bring them all together into a cohesive argument and so tends to lack focus (AO1). Some reorganisation would help and more signposts to the reader would clarify development of points. A little more close analysis is also needed, with attention to language and form (AO2). There is quite good use of historical and literary context (AO4), although it could be more integrated and developed. Discussion of alternative critical interpretations are essential and be more specific about which critic you mean (AO3).

For a B grade

- The argument needs to be clearer and more focused.
- There should be more close detailed analysis of language, form and structure.
- Historical and literary context should be relevant and integrated.
- Use some more useful quotations.
- Mention at least one specific critic's perspective.

CANDIDATE 2

AO2 Good to start with an immediate detail

When Henry recites a mock-Gothic story to entertain Catherine on the journey to Northanger Abbey, he may be ridiculing the all-too-familiar tropes of the Gothic, but Catherine is completely caught up in the tale: 'Well, what then?' she prompts, and 'Well, go on'. Like Henry, Jane Austen ridicules Gothic tropes in "Northanger Abbey", and while we may not be quite as naïve as Catherine, we too become caught up in the story at least partly because of – and not in spite of – these Gothic tropes. The tropes are not just ridiculed; they perform important functions: most notably, they create an alliance between narrator and reader, produce dramatic tension and are essential to the development of the theme of illusion and reality.

AO3 Be a little clearer about the specific genre being ridiculed

AO1 Clear statement of your position on the question

AO3 Relevant use of critic

As Katrin Burlin observes, from her aggressive opening to her 'noisy reentrance at the end' (1975, p. 38), the narrator is always there, guiding our responses to both her and the story over which she presides. In Volume One, she creates an easy intimacy with the reader precisely through her ridiculing of Gothic. Placing us on the same intellectual level as herself, she flatters us by assuming we are too sophisticated not to laugh at Catherine's naïve thoughts and Gothic visions. But the reader is actually being set up for the events at the abbey, and this is all part of the way in which Austen creates dramatic tension.

AO2 Attention to questions of structure is good

AO1 Use of detail and quotation flows nicely into your writing

Catherine's expectations of Northanger Abbey are fuelled by her reading of Gothic romance. She expects 'long, damp passages', 'narrow cells and ruined chapel', and, with a bit of luck, 'some awful memorials of an injured and ill-fated nun'. The abbey is an immediate disappointment, Gothic tropes giving way to an entirely modern home, richly furnished, full of light and comfort, and not a cobweb to be seen. We might remember Ann Radcliffe's Emily and the mystery of the black veil. Catherine's Gothic imaginings are then ridiculed here. This three-part movement from mystery to Gothic expectations to satiric anticlimax will now repeatedly recur.

AO3 Good connection, but you need to explain the reference more

AO2 Another good point about structure

AO2 Perhaps more analysis of the language here?

First, Catherine spots 'an immense heavy chest' that sparks her curiosity. Using free indirect discourse, Austen exposes the Gothic tropes which spring to Catherine's mind: the handles broken by 'some strange violence' and the 'mysterious cypher' on the lid. Anticlimax follows: the chest contains nothing but a white bedspread. Catherine subsequently scorns the 'causeless fears of an idle fancy', but within moments another mystery is posed by a black cabinet. Again Gothic tropes are exploited – the hollow 'murmurs' that seem to 'creep along the gallery' and the distant moans that chill her blood – as free indirect discourse reveals Catherine's fears and excitement. Finally, Gothic tropes are again deflated: the supposed 'manuscript' is just a washing list.

AO1 Use of critical terms

AO3 You could make reference to Gothic texts which exploit the 'found manuscript' like *The Castle of Otranto*

Dramatic tension followed by inevitable anticlimax is linked to the main themes of the novel: illusion and reality. This theme is treated satirically when, for example, the narrator wryly observes that Captain Tilney, oblivious to Catherine's charms, will not be the villain to abduct her in a chaise and four, or when Catherine is

AO1 There is some very good linking of ideas and textual detail here but this is a long sentence which is difficult to follow

'abducted' on a tourist day trip with John Thorpe – and with these incidents, the narrator appears to ridicule the trope of abduction and to insist such fantasies have little to do with everyday reality.

AO1
Use of connectives to produce coherent argument

Simultaneously, however, Gothic tropes show that the boundary between illusion and reality is actually not so well defined. Henry's send-up of Eleanor's and Catherine's misunderstanding over 'something very shocking [that] will soon come out in London' shows that the boundary between illusion and reality is more unstable than the simple ridiculing of Gothic tropes might suggest. While Henry laughs at his sister's exaggerated fears of such horrors as 'a mob of three thousand men assembling in St. George's Fields', the informed reader knows that Henry's description echoes events that have in fact already taken place: London is not immune to such 'horrors'.

AO3
Moving to an alternative position reveals ambiguity

AO4
Good moment to bring in context, but you haven't made it clear what the contextual issues really are. Repressive government? Fears of revolt?

This is an incident to recall when considering Catherine's fourth and final imagined Gothic story: the one in which the General has either locked up or murdered his wife. Many readers have found that, despite having repeatedly laughed at Catherine's expense, they now become caught up in this final Gothic tale. Perhaps this is because, as Henry Rogers argues, General Tilney is 'the only Gothic element that is not undercut or explained away until late in the novel, and his moodiness, domestic tyranny, and oppressive presence are not inconsistent with Gothic convention' (1999).

AO4
Good use of critical authority which sets you up to make your own point rather than simply making the point for you. But quotation is a bit long

If, in Volume One, we are completely distanced from Catherine and share the narrator's superior understanding, in Volume Two, the strategy begins to change. There is a mystery here, even if it is not to do with chests or cabinets. Why are Henry and Eleanor so restrained when Catherine visits, what is the tension between them and their father, and why does Catherine feel that although the General is attentive and charming, she does not enjoy his company and it is 'a release to get away from him'? As Catherine puzzles over this, so does the reader.

AO1
Nice use of rhetorical questions but another long sentence

It is Catherine's familiarity with Gothic tropes that teaches her to fear the kind of patriarchal authority that the General represents. In identifying something in his 'air and attitude' reminiscent of Lewis's Gothic villain Montoni, she is right. He was a tyrant to his wife, he is a tyrant to his daughter, and he is, like Montoni with Emily, after Catherine's money. I think therefore that Austen does not use the tropes of the Gothic purely for the purposes of ridicule; she uses them to domesticate Gothic: she brings the Gothic home.

AO3
Reference to other texts

AO1
Returns us to the main question and conveys sense of conclusion, but with an original twist

GRADE A

Comment
An excellent focus on the question, with a clear sense of developing argument (AO1). This is generally well written, though some sentences are rather long and take away from the clarity of the argument. The response pays good attention to structure, but more could be done in terms of analysing language (AO2). Useful critical viewpoints are offered and some reference to other texts (AO3) but context remains just a little too vague (AO4). All in all, however, an engaged, knowledgeable and occasionally original response.

For an A* grade
● Be more specific about the historical context that you vaguely refer to.
● Aim for more close analysis of language.
● Avoid over-long sentences, and ensure that each stage of the argument is clearly plotted out.

WORKING THROUGH A TASK

Now it's your turn to work through a task on *Northanger Abbey*. The key is to:

- Read/decode the task/question.
- Plan your points – then expand and link your points.
- Draft your answer.

TASK TITLE

How far do you agree that Austen portrays sense to be more important than sensibility in *Northanger Abbey*?

DECODE THE QUESTION: KEY WORDS

How far do you agree..?	=	what are **my** views?
Austen portrays	=	a reminder that this is a literary creation
sense	=	rational, sensible
sensibility	=	imagination, feelings

PLAN AND EXPAND

- Key aspect: evidence of the importance of sense

POINT	EXPANDED POINT	EVIDENCE
Point a *The Morland family is praised for good sense*	• *The Morlands as sensible people – initially shown as positive thing.* • *Catherine as a heroine who generally acts in a sensible manner*	Quotations 1–2 • *'Her mother was a woman of useful plain sense' (p. 15).* • *Guided only by what was simple and 'probable, it had never entered her head that Mr. Tilney could be married' (p. 52).*
Point b *Mrs Allen is satirised for lack of sense*	Different aspects of this point expanded *You fill in*	Quotations 1–2 *You fill in*
Point c *But sense is shown to have its limitations*	Different aspects of this point expanded *You fill in*	Quotations 1–2 *You fill in*

- Key aspect: evidence of importance of sensibility

You come up with three points, and then expand them

POINT	EXPANDED POINT	EVIDENCE
Point a	Different aspects of this point expanded *You fill in*	Quotations 1–2 *You fill in*
Point b	Different aspects of this point expanded *You fill in*	Quotations 1–2 *You fill in*
Point c	Different aspects of this point expanded *You fill in*	Quotations 1–2 *You fill in*

CONCLUSION

POINT	EXPANDED POINT	EVIDENCE
Key final point or overall view *You fill in*	Draw together and perhaps add a final further point to support your view *You fill in*	Final quotation to support your view *You fill in*

DEVELOP FURTHER, THEN DRAFT

Now look back over your draft points and:

- Add further links or connections between the points to develop them further or synthesise what has been said, for example:

> *Although Isabella professes to be a woman of excessive sensibility, she is in fact one of the characters most associated with sense in the novel. She is, after all, driven by very rational motives, not by her feelings, but by her economic needs.*

- Decide an order for your points/paragraphs – some may now be linked/connected and therefore **not** in the order of the table above.

Now draft your essay. If you're really stuck you can use the opening paragraph below to get you started.

> *When Henry admonishes Catherine, urging her to 'Consult your own understanding, your own sense of the probable' (p. 186), he initially appears as a voice of authority, declaring the importance of sense over sensibility, reason over imagination. But if sense should be dominant, Austen demonstrates, it needs to be tempered by sensibility, with its imaginative expansion of the mind and its empathetic understanding of others, and those characters driven purely by sense are ultimately found to be lacking. …*

Once you've written your essay, turn to page 120 for a mark scheme on this question to see how well you've done.

FURTHER QUESTIONS

1. What is the function of Austen's use of free indirect discourse in *Northanger Abbey*?

2. Austen leaves it to the reader to decide 'whether the tendency of this work be altogether to recommend parental tyranny, or reward filial disobedience'. What does she mean, and what do you think the tendency of the work is?

3. 'Isabella is the real villain of *Northanger Abbey*.' To what extent would you agree with this proposition?

4. What does *Northanger Abbey* tell us about Austen's position on reading novels?

5. What role do social conventions play in the world of *Northanger Abbey* and another text you have studied?

6. 'In terms of Gothic romance, Eleanor is far more like the typical heroine than Catherine.' To what extent do you agree with this proposition?

ESSENTIAL STUDY TOOLS

FURTHER READING

ON *NORTHANGER ABBEY*

Richard Handler and Daniel Segal, *Jane Austen and the Fiction of Culture*, Rowman &
Littlefield, 1999
For the advanced student wishing to understand more about Austen's writing in terms
of her culture

Barbara Hardy, *A Reading of Jane Austen*, Peter Owen, 1975
An early but still useful introduction to Austen

Claudia L. Johnson, *Jane Austen: Women, Politics and the Novel*, University of Chicago Press,
1988
Includes an important reading of how Austen domesticates the Gothic

Juliet McMaster, ed., *Jane Austen's Achievement*, Macmillan, 1976
Good collection of essays including Barbara Hardy on 'Properties and Possessions'

Robert Miles, *Jane Austen*, Northcote House, 2003
A short but useful introduction

Norman Page, *The Language of Jane Austen*, Oxford University Press, 1972
Still the best assessment of Austen's language and style

Tony Tanner, *Jane Austen*, Harvard University Press, 1986
Important chapter on 'Anger in the Abbey'

ON AUSTEN'S LIFE

Marilyn Butler, *Jane Austen*, Oxford University Press, 2007
A concise introduction

Claire Tomalin, *Jane Austen: A Life*, Penguin, 1997
Very readable but scholarly

HISTORICAL CONTEXT

Marilyn Butler, *Jane Austen and the War of Ideas*, Clarendon Press, 1975
Seminal work on Austen's intellectual context

Deirdre Le Faye, *Jane Austen: The World of Her Novels*, Francis Lincoln, 2003
Highly readable account of the social context

Janet Todd, ed., *Jane Austen in Context*, Cambridge University Press, 2005
Scholarly collection of essays on the historical and social contexts

LITERARY CONTEXT

Glennis Byron and Dale Townshend, eds, *The Gothic World*, Routledge, 2013
Essays on all aspects of the Gothic

Sue Chaplin, *Gothic Literature: Texts, Contexts, Connections*, York Press, 2011
Excellent introduction and highly accessible

David Lodge, *The Art of Fiction*, Penguin, 1993; Viking, 2003
Explores various fictional methods and techniques with clear examples

LITERARY TERMS

aesthetic unity   the idea, associated with the New Critics of the 1950s and 1960s, which values the richly complex unity of all parts of a work of art, all of which constitute a well-wrought whole

alliteration   the repetition of an initial consonant sound, for example, the 'b' sound in this line from *The Great Gatsby:* 'So we beat on, boats against the current, borne back ceaselessly into the past.'

anachronism   a person or thing chronologically out of place

anaphora   repeating a word or sequence of words at the start of neighbouring clauses, producing a sense of emphasis, for example, this excerpt from a speech by Winston Churchill: 'we shall fight on the landing grounds, we shall fight in the fields and in the streets, we shall fight in the hills. We shall never surrender.'

aphorism   a short pithy saying expressing a general truth, for example, Oscar Wilde's 'A man can't be too careful in the choice of his enemies.'

Bildungsroman   a coming-of-age story that follows the protagonist's psychological development, for example, *Jane Eyre* and *Great Expectations*

deus ex machina   literally, 'god from the machine': a seemingly insoluble problem is suddenly and abruptly resolved, with a contrived and unexpected introduction of a person or event

dichotomy   a division into two seemingly mutually exclusive or contradictory groups, for example, fact and fiction

Enlightenment   a term used to describe a literary and philosophical movement in Europe that had a profound faith in the powers of human reason; beginning in the late seventeenth century, it continued for much of the eighteenth century

eponymous   relating to, or being the person or thing for whom or which something is named; Jane is the eponymous heroine of Brontë's *Jane Eyre*

foreshadow   present an indication or a suggestion of what will happen in advance

free indirect style   allows the narrative voice to slip in and out of the consciousness of characters

genre   a literary type, for example, Gothic, fantasy, romance

Gothic   a genre of writing which has a number of typical elements such ghosts, horror, sublime landscapes

hyperbole   exaggeration, for example, 'I'm so hungry I could eat a horse.'

ideology   in its simplest form, a set of beliefs, a comprehensive vision, a way of looking at the world

imagery   use of language to evoke sense-impressions

irony   saying the opposite of what you mean, or inviting an interpretation different from the surface meaning of your words

juvenilia   literary, musical or artistic works produced by an author during his or her youth

metafiction   fiction that calls attention to its fictional status, commenting on the processes of composition

metaphor   a comparison between two things, without use of like or as, for example, death is a journey

metonymy   a rhetorical device in which something is defined by what is associated with it, for example, identifying the Queen as 'the Crown'

motif   a recurring element in a literary, musical or artistic work

narrator   the person, as distinct from the author, who is telling the story; the **third-person narrator** is outside the story and refers to all characters as 'he' or she'; the **omniscient narrator** knows the thoughts and feelings of all the characters; the **authorial narrator** speaks from a position of authority, conveying a sense of his or her control or ownership of the world described; the **intrusive narrator** draws attention to him- or herself through commentary, directly or indirectly addressed to the reader; the **self-conscious narrator** demonstrates an awareness that he or she is writing a book or novel, often through commentary on conventions

parody   a work that comments on another work through satiric or ironic imitation, combining creative expression with critical commentary

pastiche   a jarring combination of different conventions, tropes and discourses that aims for the absurd, and lacks the ulterior motives and satiric impulses of parody

patriarchy   a social system marked by the authority of the father and the legal and economic subordination of women

pedagogy   the science of education, the theories behind the teaching of skills and the acquisition of knowledge; something with pedagogical value is something which serves a useful educational function

picaresque   from the Spanish for 'rogue' or 'rascal', a type of fiction dealing with the episodic adventures of a usually roguish protagonist

picturesque   generally speaking, suggesting or suitable for a picture; an aesthetic ideal introduced by William Gilpin in 1782 to educate travellers in the appreciation of landscape

protagonist   leading character in a story

proverbs   popular phrases that express generally accepted truths, such as 'a cat may look at a king'

realist novel   very generally speaking, an attempt to show life 'as it is', and to use language as a transparent window to this 'real' life

rhetoric   the deliberate exploitation of eloquence for persuasive effect; a rhetorical question is asked purely for effect and without expectation of a response

romance   a narrative that departs from the dictates of reality as it is known to common sense in order to evoke a magical world

satire   a means by which vices, follies, abuses and shortcomings are held up to ridicule

symbol   something representing something else, often an idea or quality, by analogy or association

tautology   needless repetition of an idea, statement or word, for example, 'he *died* of a *fatal* overdose'

tropes   words or expressions used as figurative language or common and overused devices, for example, using the castle is a trope commonly associated with the Gothic

TIMELINE

WORLD EVENTS	AUSTEN'S LIFE	LITERARY EVENTS
	1775 Jane Austen born in Steventon, Hampshire	
1776 American Declaration of Independence		**1776** Adam Smith, *The Wealth of Nations*
		1778 Frances Burney, *Evelina*
1780 Gordon Riots in London, protesting Catholic Relief Act		
	1785 With her sister Cassandra, Austen attends Abbey School in Reading	
	1787 Austen begins writing juvenilia	**1787** Mary Wollstonecraft, *Thoughts on the Education of Daughters*
1789 French Revolution breaks out		
		1791 Ann Radcliffe, *The Romance of the Forest*
1792 September massacres: 12,000 political prisoners murdered in France; France declared a Republic		**1792** Wollstonecraft, *A Vindication of the Rights of Woman*
1793 Execution of Louis XVI and Marie Antoinette in France; start of Reign of Terror; France declares war on England		
1794 Habeas Corpus suspended in Britain		**1794** Radcliffe, *The Mysteries of Udolpho*; William Blake, *Songs of Innocence and of Experience*
1795 Seditious Meetings Act and Treasonable Practices Act		
		1796 Matthew Lewis, *The Monk*
		1797 Radcliffe, *The Italian*
		1798 William Wordsworth and Samuel Taylor Coleridge, *Lyrical Ballads*
	1801 Austen's father, Revd George Austen, retires and the family move to Bath	
1802 Napoleon appointed Consul for life	**1802** Austen accepts marriage proposal from Harris Bigg-Wither, but changes her mind next day	
1803 Britain declares war on Napoleon	**1803** 'Susan', an early version of *Northanger Abbey*, sold to publisher Crosby	
1804 Napoleon crowned Emperor	**1804** Austen writes unfinished novel, *The Watsons*	
1805 Battle of Trafalgar	**1805** Austen's father dies	
1807 Britain abolishes slave trade	**1807** Austens move to Southampton	
	1809 Austens move to Chawton, Hampshire	
1811 Luddite riots protesting against industrialisation; George, Prince of Wales, becomes Regent	**1811** Austen publishes *Sense and Sensibility*	
1812 United States declares war on Britain		
	1813 Austen publishes *Pride and Prejudice*	
1814 George Stephenson builds first locomotive engine		**1814** Walter Scott, *Waverley*
1815 Battle of Waterloo, end of Napoleonic Wars; restoration of monarchy in France	**1815** Austen publishes *Emma*	**1815** Percy Bysshe Shelley, 'Alastor'
	1816 Austen's health deteriorates; she finishes *Persuasion*; 'Susan' bought back from Crosby	
	1817 Austen dies; Henry and Cassandra oversee publication of *Northanger Abbey* ('Susan') and *Persuasion*	**1817** John Keats, *Poems*
		1818 Mary Shelley, *Frankenstein*

REVISION FOCUS TASK ANSWERS

TASK 1

In the world of *Northanger Abbey*, conventions are essential to the ordering and regulation of society.

- Conventions in terms of social behaviour – in other words, the unwritten rules and regulations regarding behaviour in public – allow the characters to identify the social status of others and to display their own.

- Eleanor is the embodiment of conventional behaviour, and also the most refined and elegant of the female characters.

- Isabella and John, on the other hand, demonstrate their vulgarity through their lack of understanding of acceptable social etiquette. While the naive Catherine does not initially recognise this, the Tilneys reject the Thorpes as their inferiors from the start.

TASK 2

Henry Tilney, as his sister says, is more 'nice' (particular) than wise in his attitude to language.

- Henry's fussiness about language often appears to be prompted by his enjoyment of teasing or making fun of others, as in this chapter when he is making fun of Catherine.

- Nevertheless, lack of precision in language can lead to confusion in communication, as the misunderstanding between Catherine and Eleanor goes on to demonstrate.

- More generally, language is so often used to deceive in *Northanger Abbey* – as in the case of Isabella's linguistic manipulations of people – that Henry's insistence on precision in the use of language also appears justified.

TASK 3

Catherine Morland is an odd heroine for an Austen novel since she is of limited understanding and even occasionally 'stupid'.

- Austen's heroines are usually much cleverer than Catherine, and if they are duped by others, so is the reader.

- Catherine frequently demonstrates a lack of understanding of other people, and is very easily manipulated by her 'friend' Isabella while the reader sees through Isabella and consequently feels superior to Catherine.

- However, Catherine is easily duped because she is the most naive of all Austen's female protagonists, and the function of the novel is to trace her social and personal development.